Beneath Your Feet: on caring for the Earth's resources

A Geography/Science topic for KS1/KS2

by Jane Bayley

A topic integrating the Environmental Change theme
of sustainability with the Materials theme

Activities including songs for children
Background notes including National Curriculum
planning guidance for teachers

Q
QUESTIONS
PUBLISHING

27 Frederick Street, Birmingham B1 3HH

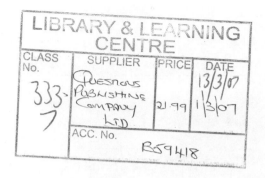
First published in 2000 by
The Questions Publishing Company Ltd
27 Frederick Street, Birmingham B1 3HH

© 2000 Jane Bayley

Song words and music © Grapevine Music,
37 Goldsmith Street, Maryborough 3465,
Victoria, Australia

Designed and typeset by Keystroke, Wolverhampton
Cover design by Martin Cater
Illustrations by Martin Cater

ISBN: 1-898149-83-6

Beneath Your Feet:
on caring for the Earth's resources

Contents

List of figures and tables

FIGURES

TABLES

List of activities and songs

ACTIVITIES

vii

SONGS

Acknowledgements

I would particularly like to express my sincere thanks to:

Olive Dyer, my colleague, whose encouragement and advice was an enormous support to me throughout the preparation of this publication. Her wisdom, thanks to many years' experience in the primary school classroom, as an advisory teacher and an author, has been invaluable.

My parents, Betty and John Bayley, for cultivating and supporting my interest in the environment from an early age and for all the many ways in which they have supported me over the years of my studies.

Authors who have generously given permission for their work to be reproduced here.

My students and pupils who have contributed so much to my understanding of the needs of teachers and children.

The staff at Questions Publishing Company for their support and tolerance.

Introduction

THE VALUE OF THIS PACK

Our very survival depends on the careful use and management of the materials that lie beneath our feet – the soils and rocks which sustain us by providing food, fuels, building materials and many other products which we rely upon in our daily lives. This publication covers those issues, which will have a lasting impact on the lives of children.

Earth materials provide a rich resource for children to explore using all their senses; many concepts will be grasped without being verbalised. Like the children, you too should be largely concerned with 'hands on' experience, and it is important to realise that a lack of specialised knowledge will not prevent you from teaching this theme effectively. This resource file has been produced in such a way that you will be able to tackle each topic with confidence.

USING THE MATERIAL

You can refer to Table 1 to help you select the most appropriate activities for your target age group, to identify learning objectives and the areas of the National Curriculum 2000 Programme of Study targeted.

You are encouraged to use the enquiry approach as a highly effective framework for planning and learning, so much of the material is presented under key questions. Frequent use is made of diagrams, including grids, for easy reference.

Key concepts have been explained at a level which should provide adequate background for teachers preparing children up to KS2. Some of the activities are suitable for KS1, whilst many are suitable for KS2. Obviously you are best able to judge how the material should be selected or modified according to the age, ability and experience of the children in your class.

The pack is divided into three sections: resources, soil, and rocks. At the beginning of each section a diagrammatic summary of the topic is presented as a means of addressing and then integrating National Curriculum geography and science statements. In the 2000 Revised Orders, many concepts relevant to these topics appear in the science document, especially under '**Materials and their properties**' and the geography document under the **Environmental Change** theme. However, there is no doubt that geography-led themes are a highly effective means of integrating a number of cross-curricular subject areas. The strength of this resource is its focus upon those new areas of the geography document relating to **Sustainable Development and the individual's responsibility for the environment.**

In this pack you will find three types of material presented for your use:

● **teacher's background:** information for reference as well as guidance on activities and an indication of key words and key skills addressed;

● **suggested activities:** for children, or for teachers to demonstrate;

● **photocopiable activity sheets.**

You will make the learning experience more valuable by placing these themes within the context of place studies; that is, related to localities in your area or an Economically Developing Country locality, or, for KS1, a contrasting locality. For KS2 all three localities must be studied.

At the end of each section are suggested assessment activities, an exemplar of how to integrate the topic into place studies and a list of resources which have proved valuable both for teachers' and children's use.

TEACHER'S BACKGROUND WHY LEARN ABOUT 'BENEATH OUR FEET'?

An understanding of the nature and value of soils and rocks is a foundation essential to the economic activities of farming, quarrying and mining, all of which feature in the National Curriculum KS2 locality studies and to a lesser extent at KS1.

If we consider our basic needs for survival – food, water, shelter and warmth – it is apparent that all of these to a greater or lesser extent are derived from 'beneath our feet': food comes from plants which grow in soil or from the animals which eat those plants; water from underground (97 per cent of fresh water is found there); building materials for our homes; and fuels for warmth and cooking. Of course, in our developed society we put a much greater strain upon the Earth's limited resources by our high consumption of a wide variety of mineral and rock resources.

Thus it is important that children gain an understanding of the concepts of the vast periods of time taken for these resources to form and thus of non-sustainable resource use. From this they will appreciate the need to recycle, reuse, repair, return, restore or reduce use in order to conserve resources for the future, as highlighted in the Environmental Change theme of the 2000 Geography Order.

One of the most effective ways of putting these ideas across to children is through practical activities in the school and its grounds or, at KS2, in the wider local area, finding out what is 'beneath their feet' and then considering how they or others have used or are using the soil and rock resources. Finally, they might consider how the resources could be better used in future. These activities fit neatly into *Local Agenda 21* objectives which address sustainability at a local level. Agenda 21 is a document, signed by 151 governments at the 1992 Earth Summit, which describes the policies needed for sustainable development in the 21st century, a theme which features heavily in the Revised National Curriculum (2000) Geography Orders.

Here is a useful proverb which reminds of the need to save our resources for future generations:

'We do not inherit the earth from our parents
It is lent to us by our children.'

Table 1 A summary of the children's activities, their intended target group, learning objectives and National Curriculum coverage.

Activity	Target Year Group	Learning Objectives	Science POS	Geog. POS	Page
RESOURCES					
Will it last?	Years 5–6	to understand the concepts of renewable resources	S1.1, 1.3, 2.3	1.1, 1.3, 1.4, 3.2	13
The six Rs	Years 5–6	to introduce ways of reducing waste of the Earth's resources	S1.1	1.1, 1.4, 3.2, 3.5	14
Ways of saving the Earth's resources	Years 5–6	to raise awareness of the most beneficial actions to reduce resource waste	S1.1	1.1, 1.3, 1.4, 3.1, 3.2, 3.4, 3.5	16
Recycling Song	Years 1–6	to reinforce methods of recycling	*S1.1, 1.3* S1.1, 1.3	2.7, 3.2, 3.5	17
Choosing to save resources	Years 3–4 Years 5–6	to raise awareness of the impact of contrasting consumer habits		1.1, 1.3,1.4, 2, 3.1, 3.2, 3.4, 3.5	18
Sustainable shopping	Years 5–6	to raise awareness of the origin of supermarket products and their relative sustainability		1.1, 1.3, 1.4, 3.1, 3.2, 3.4, 3.5	19
Certificate	Years 1–6	to state intended actions to conserve resources		1.4, 3.1, 3.2, 3.4, 3.5	21
Waste monster	Years 3–4 Years 5–6	to take action to promote recycling	S1.1	1.4, 3.1, 3.2, 3.5	21
Design a recycling centre	Years 5–6	to design and promote recycling	S1.1	1.4, 1.7, 3.2, 3.5	23
Poster design	Years 3–6	to consolidate learning on why recycling is necessary		3.1, 3.2, 3.4, 3.5	24
What can we do to help?	Years 3–6	to consolidate learning on saving resources		1.4, 2, 3.1, 3,2	25
SOILS					
Soil recipes	Years 1–6	to understand what soil is made of	*S1.1, M1.1, M1.3* S1.1 M1.4		31
Soils and the senses	Years 1–6	to recognise the similarities and differences between soils	*1.1, 1.2, 1.3, M1.1, M1.2, M1.3* S1.1, 1.2, 1.3, M1.1		32

Key: Under the Science POS, S = Scientific Enquiry POS; M = Materials and their properties; italicised references relate to KS1

Title	Years	Objective	Science Enquiry (S) references	Other references	Page
Soil Ain't Dirt Song	Years 3–6	to appreciate the value of soil and its fragility		3.1, 3.2, 3.5	33
Making a soil pit	Years 3–4 Years 5–6	to observe changes in soil with depth	S1.1, 1.2, 1.3	1.1, 1.2, 1.4, 1.5, 2.2, 2.6	37
Soil paints Mother Earth	Years 3–6) Years 1–6)	to record and display changes in the soil with depth	S1.2, 1.3, 2.2, 2.5 *1.1, 1.2, 1.3, 2.1, 2.2, 2.4, M1.1, 1.3* S1.2, 1.3, 2.2, 2.5	1.4, 2.6	38
The Sherlock Holmes Mystery	Years 5–6	to apply knowledge of changes in soil characteristics with depth	S1.1, 1.2, 3.12		39
Is my soil acid?	Years 5–6	to observe and record results of an experiment	S1.1, 3.11, 3.12, 3.13	2.6	42
Making soil doughnuts Settling jar	Years 5–6) Years 5–6)	to investigate the proportion of sand, silt and clay in soils	S1.1, 1.4, M3.1	2.6	43
Earthworm Song	Years 3–6	to appreciate the importance of living things in the soil	S1.1, 1.3, M2.1		45
Rotter's Restaurant	Years 5–6	to extend understanding of mini-beasts in decomposition	S1.1, 1.3, M2.1		47
Wormery	Years 2–6	to observe the action of worms in the soil over a period of time	*S1.1, 1.2, 1.3,* S1.1, 1.2, S1.3, 2.1, 3		48
A leaf's life	Years 3–6	to develop understanding of the cycling of plant materials	S1.1, 1.3, 2.1		49
The Compost Makers' Worksong; compost and compost heaps	Years 5–6) Years 5–6)	to understand how decay leads to recycling of nutrients to produce a fertiliser when adequate moisture, air and temperatures are supplied	S1.1, 1.3, 2.1 S1.1, 1.2, 1.3, 2.1, 2.2, 3		50
Land Links Song	Years 1–4	to explain that most products are derived from natural resources from the land		2.6, 2, 3.2	58
The wearing wind	Years 5–6	to investigate soil erosion by wind	S1, 2.1, 2.2, 3, M3.1	3.1, 3.2	63
The story of Mr Marram and Mr Sand	Years 5–6	to illustrate the importance of vegetation in reducing wind erosion and the effect of trampling in destroying vegetation	S1, 2, M3.1	3.1, 3.2	65
The wicked water	Years 5–6	to investigate erosion by water	S1, 2, 3	3.1, 3.2	73
The soil squashers	Years 5–6	to investigate the impact of compaction in soil	S1, 2, 3	3.1, 3.2	75
Mud in our school	Years 5–6	to investigate soil erosion in the school grounds	S1, 2, 3	2, 3.1, 3.2, 3.5	76

Key: Under the Science POS, S = Scientific Enquiry POS; M = Materials and their properties; italicised references relate to KS1

Table 1 continued

Activity	Target Year Group	Learning Objectives	Science POS	Geog. POS	Page
Solving soil mysteries I Solving soil mysteries II	Years 5–6) Years 5–6)	to reinforce work on clayey and sandy soils, soil pits and soil erosion	S1, 2, 3, M1, 2		83
Planning for the future The Soil Doctor: S.O.S. – Save Our Soils!	Years 5–6) Years 5–6)	to reinforce work on threats to soils	S1.1	3.1, 3.2, 3.5	85
ROCKS					
Building a rock village	Years 2–6	to introduce the variety of rocks which exist	S1.1, 1.3, M1.1, M1.4		91
Fossil flick book	Years 5–6	to explain sedimentary rock formation and fossilisation	S1.1, 1.3		92
Feely box	Years 1–6	to distinguish rocks from other materials	*S1, 2.1, M1.1, M1.2, M1.3,* S1.1, 1.3, M1.1, M1.4		95
Stone stores and pencil pots	Years 1–6	to classify rocks	*S1, M1.1, M1.2, M1.3,* S1.1, 1.3, M1.1, M1.4		95
Where's my partner?	Years 1–6	to classify rocks, giving explanations	*S1, M1.1, M1.2, M1.3,* S1.1, 1.3, M1.1, M1.4		95
Reading with Rocky Rex	Years 5–6	to understand where rocks are found, what they are used for and to promote fieldwork safety	S1.1, 3.6	2, 3.1, 3.2	96
Model of hidden rocks	Years 5–6	to appreciate that rocks are often hidden by superficial materials	S1.1	1.2	105
Earth construction: apple analogy	Years 5–6	to understand the nature of the Earth's interior	S1.1		105

Key: Under the Science POS, S = Scientific Enquiry POS; M = Materials and their properties; italicised references relate to KS1

Title	Years	Objective	Science POS		Page
This is your life	Years 5–6	to understand the rock cycle	S1.1	2	105
Something geological is cooking!	Years 5–6	to understand how rocks and fossils are formed	S1, 2, 3, M2		107
Matching materials	Years 3–4 (intro) Years 5–6	to recognise raw and manufactured materials and match the original and altered materials	S1, M1.1, M1.4		109
Matching materials and uses	Years 5–6	to match raw materials and their uses	S1, 1.1, 1.4		110
Clay sedimentation test	Years 5–6	to carry out an investigation to determine whether a local clay is suitable for making tiles, bricks or pottery	S1, M3.1		111
Rock around the house	Years 3–4 (intro) Years 5–6	to understand that raw materials for many everyday objects come from rocks and that the materials used have changed over time	S1, M1.1, M1.4		116
Build your own home!	Years 3–4 (intro) Years 5–6	to reinforce work on materials and the properties which determine their use	S1,M1.1	3.2, 3.5	123

Key: Under the Science POS, S = Scientific Enquiry POS; M = Materials and their properties; italicised references relate to KS1

PART 1

Resources

What is a resource?

A resource is a material which is of economic value to mankind: soil, water, oil, ores, building stone, and so on. You will find a great deal more material on the subject of soil and rock resources in the later sections of the book.

Why is it worth studying resources?

Most of the objects we use in our daily life are made largely from raw materials from the Earth's crust. By extracting, transporting and processing these materials, we cause an adverse effect upon the environment. If children are able to understand their impact as consumers, they will be in a position to make informed choices, and we know that many will act in a responsible manner as a result of their knowledge and understanding.

What happens when the rocks we use run out?

You can draw children's attention to worked-out mines and quarries in their home area. Are there any reasons for closure, such as dangers of working the quarry, or new substitutes, such as tiles instead of slates? So what are tiles made from? Clay, which is another natural resource. But we need to bear in mind that to make tiles from clay, fossil fuel is required both to bake the tiles and transport them to market, so wasting more precious resources (see pp. 13).

What could children learn?

A logical teaching sequence might be:

1. Investigation of mining and quarrying

   To explore **case studies**, preferably local field studies of the extractive industries of mining and quarrying, and associated manufacturing industry and waste disposal. This is such an important industry in the UK: on average we consume 6 tonnes of rock per head annually. Some examples follow:

● Table 2 which gives general principles that might be demonstrated in local studies.

● Children should be asked to express their **likes and dislikes** of these sites and, at KS2, to discuss how the environment can be looked after or managed including that some environments need special protection, e.g. National Parks.

2. Greening of lifestyles

   To identify how children's lifestyles might be changed in order to lessen their impact on the environment.

Table 2 The effects of extracting resources from the Earth: Teacher's background

Key questions	Mining	Quarrying	Manufacturing industry	Waste disposal
How is it done?	Digging materials from underground e.g. coal, gold.	Digging materials from the Earth's surface e.g. open cast coal, limestone, clay, sand and gravel.	Using energy, water, machinery and labour etc. to make cement from limestone and clay or gold from gold ore.	Usually burying the waste (landfill). Less commonly by incineration.
Where is it done?	The more valuable the resource, the deeper it's worth digging for it.	Ideally, near to the market. If the material is cheap, it must be close to the market otherwise the cost of transport over a long distance would make it uneconomic to extract.	Lots of different places because there are lots of different reasons. Explore each case individually.	In old quarries or on salt marshes. Nowadays, it's often a problem finding a site near to towns.
What effect does it have on the environment?	Subsidence. Waste (spoil) at the surface. These heaps maybe unstable. Polluted water, e.g. acid water from coal mines.	Noise and dust pollution.	'Heavy' industry, such as the chemical and metal industries, causes pollution of air, land and water. 'Light' industry causes little damage except indirectly in the materials it uses.	Water flowing through the waste may wash out dangerous chemicals which may enter water supply. Methane gas is generated and may cause explosions or be used as an energy source.
How can the land be restored afterwards?	Subsidence – compensation paid. It is often possible, though difficult, to establish vegetation on spoil heaps.	For example, sand and gravel pits flood naturally and may be used for recreation or wildlife reserves.	Do not usually close due to resources becoming exhausted like mines and quarries. If closure occurs for other reasons, land may be put to other uses e.g. garden festivals or industry.	Covered with soil and vegetation re-established. It is becoming commoner now to develop 'piggyback' sites where a tip is built on top of an older one, creating a hill.

Renewable and non-renewable resources

The following ideas are basic to the understanding of saving non-renewable resources and will be useful as a basis for discussion using the principles of Scientific Enquiry specified in the 2000 Revised Order, even though the content – fuels – no longer features in the National Curriculum until KS3.

You can use the sequence of questions in Table 3 to help children to understand the concept of renewable and non-renewable resources and fossil fuels.

Table 3   Will it last? Teacher's background to activity

Questions	Answers
What makes plants grow?	Food, water, sunlight
What makes animals grow?	Eating plants or animals which ate plants and drank water. These are plants' and animals' fuels.
What is a fossil?	Something which was once alive and is now buried in the Earth's crust.
What's a fossil fuel?	Something which we get energy from, which has been buried in the Earth's crust for many millions of years. It's a sort of 'preserved sunshine': it has stored the sun's energy from a long, long time ago in the form of coal (dead plants) or gas and oil (dead plants and animals).
How do we know it's old?	It has been buried deeply in the Earth's crust. Oil, for example, is obtained from over 3km deep in the North Sea.
Will fossil fuels run out?	Yes! There is still much coal in the crust but oil and gas are becoming scarce. We're using them very very much faster than new resources form so we say that they are non-renewable: one day they will run out.
Can you name any renewable sources of energy – those that we can continue using because they won't run out?	Sun, which causes wind (as air flows between places of different temperatures), waves which are caused by the wind, tides and heat in the Earth's crust (there's so much that it won't run out). However, the hot rocks are often rather deep, though they are shallow in some places where there are volcanoes.

Refuse Refuse!

Think of the 2 different meanings and pronunciations of this word.

We can refuse to waste the Earth's resources so that we don't produce so much refuse (rubbish). You can tell children that waste disposal costs their school, the community and the environment a great deal; they could be asked to think of ways of reducing waste. Can they think of any words beginning with the letter 'R' which might help? Six words are shown in bold in Figure 1. To help the children remember these, the game in Figure 2 could be used. More able children might then attempt the activity sheet, Figure 3. Some suggested responses are shown in Figure 1 below. This activity could be used to lead into a project on improving the environment at school (or elsewhere).

The 'Recycling Song' (see p. 17) will provide entertainment and links nicely with composting, which is discussed on pp. 56 and 57 in the soils section.

Did you know?

Recycling four milk bottles or eight drinks cans save one litre of fuel oil? Using rechargeable batteries saves both materials and cost – in the long term, they are a fraction of the cost of disposable batteries.

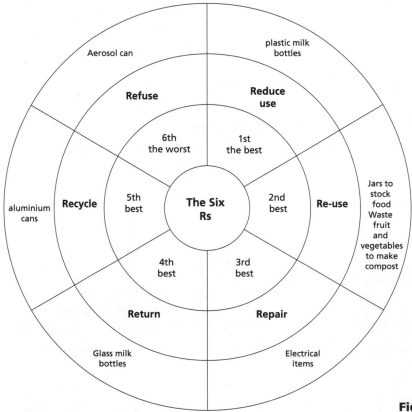

Figure 1 The six Rs

Figure 2

A GAME TO REMIND YOU OF THE SIX Rs

See if you can remember the words using the following clues:

Clues	Words
RE 	RE _____
RE 	RE _____
RE 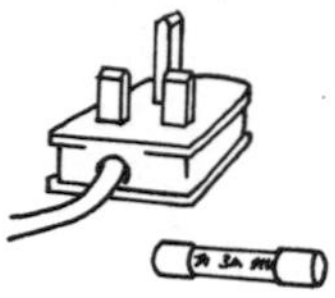 DANGER! Electricity A _ _ _ _ has blown	RE _____
RE U U U u u u	RE _____
RE 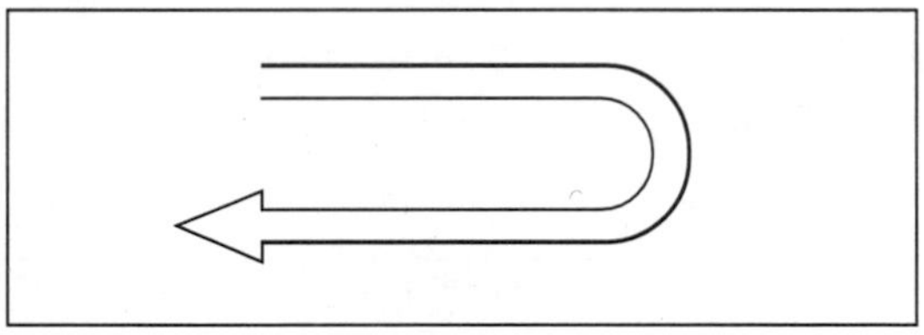	RE _____
RE  score 40 – 40	RE _____

A GAME TO REMIND YOU OF THE SIX Rs

Figure 3

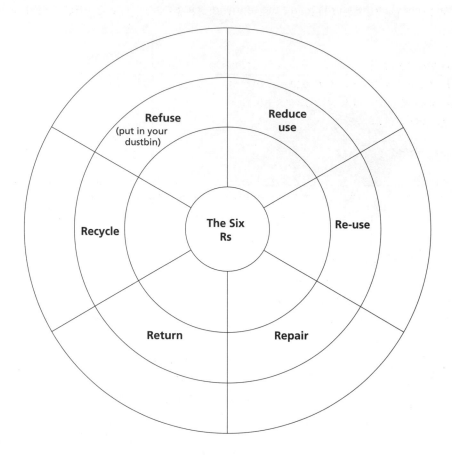

WAYS OF SAVING THE EARTH'S RESOURCES

(Diagram labels: The Six Rs (centre); Refuse (put in your dustbin), Reduce use, Recycle, Re-use, Return, Repair)

1. In the outer blank circle fill in examples of actions that we can take to save the Earth's resources: repair, return, recycle, re-use, reduce use of or, if we have no alternative, put in the dustbin. Here are some items: aluminium cans, glass milk bottles, glass jars, aerosol cans, newspapers, waste fruit and vegetables.

2. Which of the 6 Rs do you think does least harm to the environment?
   Think about which does no damage because nothing is extracted from the Earth and no waste is produced.

3. In the inner blank circle mark as number 1 the action which does the least harm; mark as number 6 the action which does the most harm, and so on.

4. Write below why you chose to put the actions in this order.

RECYCLING SONG

(To be sung to the tune of 'What shall we do with the drunken sailor?')

What shall we do with our old glass bottles,
What shall we do with our old glass bottles,
What shall we do with our old glass bottles,
Early in the morning?

Bring them to the bottle bank, RECYCLE,
Bring them to the bottle bank, RECYCLE,
Bring them to the bottle bank, RECYCLE,
Early in the morning!

Where shall we take our carrot peelings,
Where shall we take our carrot peelings,
Where shall we take our carrot peelings,
Early in the morning?

Put them on the compost heap, RECYCLE,
Put them on the compost heap, RECYCLE,
Put them on the compost heap, RECYCLE,
Early in the morning!

What shall we do with our old newspapers,
What shall we do with our old newspapers,
What shall we do with our old newspapers,
Early in the morning?

Take them to the paper-bank, RECYCLE,
Take them to the paper-bank, RECYCLE,
Take them to the paper-bank, RECYCLE,
Early in the morning!

What shall we do with the litter-throwers,
What shall we do with the litter-throwers,
What shall we do with the litter-throwers,
Early in the morning?

Drop 'em on the compost heap, RECYCLE,
Drop 'em on the compost heap, RECYCLE,
Drop 'em on the compost heap, RECYCLE,
Early in the morning!

© Judith Nicolls 1993, first printed in *Earthways, Earthwise* compiled by Judith Nicolls, published by Oxford University Press. Reprinted by permission of the author.

What happens if we forget the six Rs?

Ask the children to consider what happens if we forget the six Rs. Broadly the effects are:

- more extraction of resources, i.e. more quarries and mines;

- more waste to dispose of, i.e. more landfill sites and incinerators;

- more transport of resources, products and waste with the consequent problems of road congestion, air pollution and fossil fuel depletion;

- more pollution of the environment in processing.

Suggested activity: Choosing to save resources

In order to assist understanding of the concept, you could ask the children to compare the impact of eating a meal in a fast food restaurant with the impact of cooking a meal from fresh produce from closer to home. For an example of some of the points which might emerge in discussion see Table 4. Similar activities could be designed on these lines, e.g. transport choices (a bicycle or a car?) or clothes choices (a local woollen jumper or an oil-derived acrylic jumper made in the Far East?).

Table 4 Food choices

	A bad option	**A good option**
	A beefburger from a fast-food restaurant.	Home-cooked (partly) home-grown meal.
Ingredients and their origin	Beef from Brazil (tropical rainforest cleared to create pasture) onions from Spain; grain from Canada, refined to white flour and made into bread.	Fresh fruit and vegetables from the garden or local farmers; locally or home-produced eggs, meat or cheese.
Processing, transport and packaging costs	High (travelled across Atlantic and from Europe).	None / low.
Waste	A lot: sachets, polystyrene cup and tray, plastic knives and forks to rubbish tip.	Very little: Fruit and vegetable peelings and paper bags recycled to compost bin to improve soil fertility for next year's crop.
Effects on health	Low in fibre and high in fat. Low in vitamins. Higher risk of degenerative diseases (eg: heart disease and cancer).	Whole vegetables – higher in fibre and vitamins. Lower risk of degenerative diseases.

You will find that children can benefit from being asked to look for goods which support sustainable development. It is becoming increasingly easy to find goods which are produced in this way.

Suggested activity

Next time you go shopping, see how many goods you can find which are organic, conservation grade or fairly traded. Good places to look are your local Oxfam shop, wholefood shop and supermarket. Some of the goods which you could look for include: tea, coffee, herbal teas, chocolate, corn-flakes, butter, yoghurt, fruit and vegetables. If you buy any of these goods, save the packaging to make a display at school. There is a photocopiable activity on this topic on p. 20.

Table 5 Some definitions

Concept	Definition
Sustainable development	Development which enables us to improve our quality of life now without damaging the planet for the future.
Organic	Produced on farms that do not make use of chemical pesticides or fertilisers.
Conservation grade	Produced on farms that are partly halfway between organic and conventional chemical farms.
Fairly traded	A fair price is given to producers of these products and there may, in addition, be support given to community projects and investment.
Out of season	For example, crops which we can grow out of doors in summer in Britain. We extend the season by using heating – in a greenhouse – or importing the product from a part of the world with a warmer climate during our winter. (For example, a country in the southern hemisphere which is enjoying its summer, e.g. New Zealand, which is close to the equator; or a warm country in the northern hemisphere, e.g. Morocco.)

SUSTAINABLE SHOPPING: SHOP TO SAVE THE EARTH AND ITS PEOPLE!

When you go shopping, look at the labels to find out where the products come from. Some of the products which are often interesting are green beans, tomatoes, lettuce, apples, coffee and tea. Find out if they could be produced closer to Britain or in Britain. Is the product out of season? Record your findings on the table below.

Product	Produced in	Can it be produced closer to home?	Is it out of season?
green beans			
tomatoes			
lettuce			
apples			
coffee			
tea			

When you have finished your table, use an atlas to find out which products have travelled the furthest and record your findings below. Write a sentence to explain why it's best to buy products from closer to home.

HOW MIGHT YOU END THE TOPIC?

Suggested activities

The following can be very rewarding ways to end the unit of study:

1. to present children with a certificate stating that they now understand better how they can help to look after the earth's resources. Design the certificate to provide them with a space in which they can indicate what they intend to do to this end.

2. Read the cartoon below, then produce a Waste Monster, to encourage others to modify their behaviour: see Figure 4b on page 22.

Figure 4a   Illustrations by Steve Weatherill.

Figure 4b

The following pages (pages 23–25) give examples of activities which you can photocopy for use in end-of-term assessments.

DESIGN YOUR OWN HOME OR SCHOOL RECYCLING CENTRE!

Imagine that you have been asked by your parents or head teacher to design a recycling zone for disposal of tins, aluminium cans, waste fruit and vegetable matter, paper, glass, old clothes, plastics and oil.

Draw a plan of the part of your home or school where you plan to set up your recycling centre, naming on a key the different materials which you'd collect in each place. Remember to place them conveniently!

POSTER DESIGN

Design a poster to remind everyone to use your recycling centre. It would be useful if you explained WHY it is good to recycle so that they will feel that they want to help.

WHAT CAN WE DO TO HELP SAVE RESOURCES?

Can you fill in the table below to show what you have learnt about saving resources?

Material	What it comes from	A place where it comes from	What can be done to help save this material

TEACHING RESOURCES IN THE CONTEXT OF PLACE STUDIES

The table below gives an example of how you can use the topic resources as part of a scheme of work on place studies, at Key Stages 1 and 2. Most schools are likely to be situated in densely populated areas, where it will become obvious to children that the large population depends on resources brought in *from* places outside, and on the disposal of waste materials *to* places outside. However, you might find that columns one and two in Table 6 may need to be transposed for some schools. At KS2, the study of resources could be tied in with the study of economic activity.

Table 6 Teaching resources at KS1 and 2

	Local area	Contrasting UK locality	Less economically developed locality
KS1	Investigation of use of resources and disposal of waste in school and its grounds.	A contrasting school (a linked school) where similar or different issues apply.	Compare and contrast resources used in less developed societies.
	Wider local area	**Contrasting locality**	**Less economically developed locality**
KS2	Study of local recycling centre and waste disposal (landfill site and/or incinerator.)	Study of a rural area where recycling centres are less viable due to the lower population density.	Poor people making a living from rubbish – e.g. making sandals from old rubber tyres. The lure of western consumption.

RECOMMENDED TEACHING RESOURCES

1. *Ecoschools*: an excellent participating whole-school project run by the Tidy Britain Group, The Pier, Wigan, WN3 4EX. Tel: 01942 824620. One free set of A4 booklets on this scheme to each school.

2. *I'm writing to tell you about . . .* by Olive Dyer and Val Scurlock © 2000 GAA, Centre of Education Studies, Old College, Aberystwyth. A resource pack to interpret environmental change in the KS2 geography POS. Five case studies from Wales, including CD-ROM on reducing waste. This pack is also available in Welsh: *Annwyl Blant, A glywsoch chi sôn am . . .*

3. *Lessons in life: resources for primary school teachers, enhancing the curriculum now and in the future.* Free resource pack from Bankside. Tel: 01635 31721.

4. The Worldwide Fund for Nature: subscribe to *Lifelines*, the excellent termly newsletter available free of charge from the WWF's Education and Awareness Department. This contains a host of very good practical activities and information. *Sustainable Futures* is part of their *Reaching Out* programme. Details from WWF UK, Panda House, Weyside Park, Godalming, Surrey GU17 1XR.

5. *What a Load of Rubbish* by Steve Kidmore, *Get Switched On* by Thompson Yardley, and *Buy Now, Pay Later* by Thompson Yardley, all part of the colourful, beautifully illustrated, entertaining *Spaceship Earth* series, published by Cassell at £3.99 (paperback).

6. The National Centre for Alternative Technology, Machynlleth, Powys, SY20 9AZ (tel: 01654 702948) demonstrates energy conservation, compost making and many other aspects of green lifestyles very effectively. The 'Mole Hole' is a fascinating experience which teaches children about life in the soil. The quarterly magazine *Green Teacher* produced here is a valuable source of ideas and information.

7. *The Environmental Activities Box*, (1993) available from Northamptonshire Science Centre, Spencer House, Lewis Rd., Northampton NN5 7BJ. Tel: 01604 756134.

8. *Wake up to what you can do for the environment*, Dept of Environment. One of a number of resources produced by Waste Watch, 24 Holborn Viaduct, London EC1A 2BN. Also available is the Dustbin Pack, and an information service about waste, Wasteline, 10am–6pm. Tel: 0207 248 0242: www.wastewatch.org.uk

9. Your local recycling officer: you can arrange school visits and receive information about local initiatives.

10. EZone. CD-ROM on environmental issues BBC/Environment Agency Wales. In Welsh and English. For BBC Resources tel: 01222 322512.

11. *Lucy's World*, by Steve Weatherill. Beautifully illustrated introduction to environmental issues and how to get involved for KS1, £4. This and a number of other useful resources are available from the *Green Bookshelf* catalogue available from: Friends of the Earth, Freepost, 56-58 Alma Street, Luton, LU1 2YZ.

12. *Rescue Mission Planet Earth*, most attractive and colourful explanation of the issues discussed at the Earth Summit as interpreted by children. Available from Kingfisher Press.

PART 2

Soils

TEACHER'S BACKGROUND SOILS: AREN'T WE LUCKY TO HAVE THIS TREASURE!

The very name of our planet, Earth, reminds us that we should treasure our soil (earth), the resource without which we would not be able to produce food. By contrast, the Moon has no soil because its atmosphere is so thin – craters produced hundreds of millions of years ago still look new. The water and gases in the earth's atmosphere help to break down the rocks on the Earth's surface. Plants such as mosses and lichens also assist the breakdown by producing powerful acids such as nitric acid.

What is soil?

Soil is the medium in which plants grow because it can store water, air, plant food and warmth (though it does take a long time to gain and lose heat). It's a 'life factory' – all living things on land depend on it.

How does it form?

Suggested activity: Soil recipes

You can have fun demonstrating how to make soil using the ingredients below in the proportions shown in Figure 5. If you mix each of the ingredients shown below, you should have good soil after approximately 200 years! The importance of each ingredient needs to be emphasised: e.g. air for the animals such as worms to breathe, water for the plants and animals, animals to break down the dead organic matter to humus, and to make tunnels for air and water to pass through, minerals and humus to provide plant food, and humus to hold moisture and to bind the soil together.

    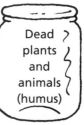

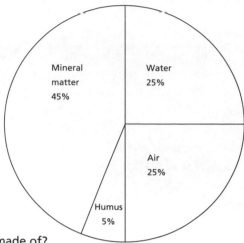

Figure 5 What is good soil made of?

Suggested activity: Soils and the senses

This activity works best when done orally in small groups with the teacher directing the questioning. Sandy and clayey soils make useful contrasts. Most children love playing with soil and they can be given dry and wetted samples of sand and clay (and possibly peat) and asked to describe:

1. Colours

2. The 'feel' of the soils: gritty, silky, soft, sticky

3. The smell of the soils

4. The weight of the soils

5. The behaviour of the soils when handled. Which makes the best 'castles'? Which might be dangerous to walk on?

6. Which dirties the hands or clothes?

The song 'Soil Ain't Dirt', on page 33, will help to reinforce concepts in the activities 'Soil recipes' and 'Soils and the senses'.

SOIL AIN'T DIRT

When you look at the ground you might see
Nothin' but dust
Flat, brown and boring – nothin' special
You might detest dust when it gets on your clothes
Curse it when it gets up your nose

Or when you touch the ground you might feel
Nothin' but dirt
Gritty and grimy – your mother doesn't like it – no
So let me introduce you to soil

Soil is amazing, it keeps us alive
Would you believe without it we could not
    survive?
Fair dinkum! This might come as a shock
But there is nothin' between our life and solid
    rock but soil

Soil is actually full of energy
Enough living power to grow a mighty tree
And it's teeming with life, microbes of every kind
You see it through a microscope, it's gonna blow your mind

Soil may stretch out for hectares around
But underneath your feet it's just a few metres down
And it's precious! one centimetre could take
Between a hundred and a thousand years to
    make!

Yeah but – soil can be damaged
It's like you or I
If it's knocked around or poisoned it can sicken
    or die

And neglected, disrespected, it can be badly hurt –
So don't treat the soil
No don't treat the soil
Don't treat the living soil like – dirt!

Soil Ain't Dirt

Medium Swing   Words & music: Fay White

Safety note for all activities involving handling of soil

Unless you are certain that children have an up-to-date tetanus vaccination, gloves should be worn when handling soil. At the very least all open wounds must be fully covered with a waterproof plaster to avoid the danger of tetanus, which is most likely to develop from stab wounds.

Suggested activity: Making a soil pit

Once the children's interest in the soil is stimulated, they will be keen to explore where it 'comes from' or 'goes to', so the next logical step is to dig a pit to find out. It is also a good observation exercise to notice the sometimes subtle changes in the soil with depth.

1. Choose a site where the soil has not been disturbed, particularly avoiding any shallow underground pipes or electricity cables. A good site can often be found on the edge of woodland. You may be able to save the trouble of digging at all if you're lucky enough to have a ready-made exposure in recently made road cuttings, stream banks, ditches or other excavations.

2. Equipment:

   ● A spade (stainless steel is the easiest type to work with)
   ● Markers to mark boundaries between layers, e.g. strips of plastic cut from discarded cartons
   ● Sheets of newspaper
   ● A tape measure

   If you are able to make the pit a permanent feature you'll also need a sturdy cover to keep the light out, a piece of clear, rigid plastic or glass and some wooden pegs to hold it in place over the vertical face.

3. Cut a square about 1m x 1m and lift off the plants and their roots in sections, placing them carefully into newspaper.

4. Dig a pit to depth of about 60cm or until you reach solid rock, placing each layer of soil on separate numbered sheets of newspaper.

5. Clean the side of the pit which faces the sun, forming a good vertical surface with a trowel or knife so that there are no smears of soil which have fallen from above.

6. The soil from each layer can be examined both in the pit and from the newspaper piles. Notice the size of particles, the colour of the soil and how wet or dry it is. The activities which follow show the characteristics of these particles in more detail.

7. Do be sure to replace the layers and the turf exactly as you found them.

Children can begin to appreciate at this stage that there are two sources of soil materials: the living things on or near the surface; and the mineral matter below. Observing how rocks can crumble to produce smaller particles, like those that are found deeper in the soil, can help children to understand the more difficult concept that soil can also be formed from below (see Figure 6).

1. Dark brown topsoil is coloured by decayed organic matter (**humus**), which is dark in colour due to its high carbon content.

2. If the topsoil is black, light in weight and highly absorbent, it is probably **peat**. This is organic matter that has only partially decayed. It occurs in waterlogged conditions, where few decomposers can live due to the shortage of oxygen. You should be able to see the remains of mosses, heathers' woody stalks, and so on, but no rock fragments.

3. The subsoil colour is governed more closely by the underlying geology – that is the parent material from which it has been formed by weathering. This can consist of solid rock, or of softer deposits such as those laid down by ice (see Figure 8). For example, if the underlying rock is limestone, and more especially, chalk, then the soil may be whitish. If the underlying rock is 'red' sandstone the soil may be brownish red/orange.

4. In wet upland moorland areas of Britain the subsoil may have two distinct layers: an upper layer which has been 'bleached' by acidic waters percolating through and removing materials rich in iron; and a lower layer where those iron-rich materials have been redeposited. Where this happens, a hard rusty '**iron pan**' is formed just above the parent material (see Figure 9).

Suggested activity: Soil paints from the soil pit

Children will enjoy recording their findings from the soil pit. Variations in colour are often subtle and are best contrasted by taking a small amount of soil, mixing it with water and using it as a 'soil paint' to record the sequence of layers found in a soil pit as a soil profile (see Figure 6).

Note: Wetting soils usually makes them noticeably darker. Children could then draw some plants at the surface and solid rock below, and add labels to summarise some of the things they have discovered.

Suggested activity: Mother Earth display

An enjoyable way of following up the soil-pit activity is to use the material excavated to make a 'Mother Earth' wall display (see Figure 7).

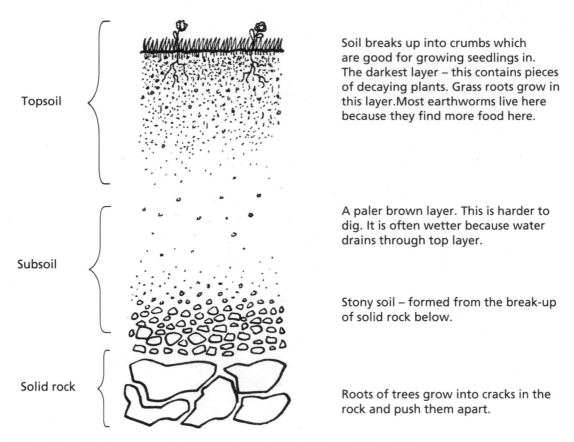

Topsoil — Soil breaks up into crumbs which are good for growing seedlings in. The darkest layer – this contains pieces of decaying plants. Grass roots grow in this layer.Most earthworms live here because they find more food here.

Subsoil — A paler brown layer. This is harder to dig. It is often wetter because water drains through top layer.

Stony soil – formed from the break-up of solid rock below.

Solid rock — Roots of trees grow into cracks in the rock and push them apart.

Figure 6 The soil profile from our soil pit (with labels which children might add)

Suggested activity: The Sherlock Holmes mystery

A 'whodunit' mystery story can be great fun to investigate. Here is an example on which you can base an activity:

There's been a mysterious death. The victim who was found lying in the bottom of a trench (which had been prepared to lay a new water pipe), had had his wallet and gold watch stolen. You have access to the shoes of the suspect. Describe how you might use your knowledge of soils to show that he is guilty of having climbed into the trench.

The key point for the children to identify here is that if the suspect is guilty of having climbed in the trench he will have picked up some of the subsoil exposed in the trench on his shoes.

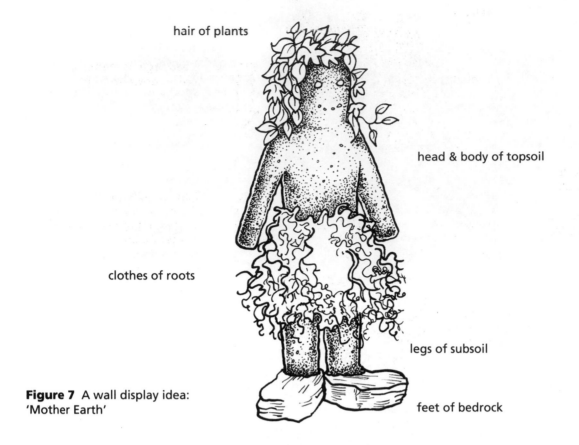

hair of plants

head & body of topsoil

clothes of roots

legs of subsoil

Figure 7 A wall display idea: 'Mother Earth'

feet of bedrock

TEACHER'S BACKGROUND
WHAT DIFFERENT TYPES OF SOIL ARE THERE?

Soil profiles and acidity of soils

In studying contrasting localities, children are likely to explore a lowland and an upland area of Britain. Figures 8 and 9 show what they are likely to find.

Worms mix the layers so vertical changes are gradual (see Rotter's Restaurant on p. 47 for further information on soil mixing by organisms).

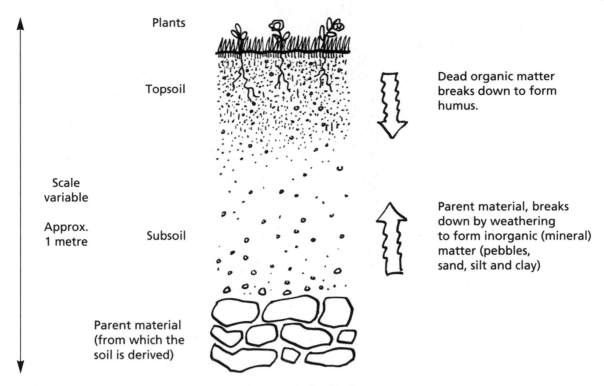

Plants

Topsoil

Scale
variable

Approx.
1 metre

Subsoil

Parent material
(from which the
soil is derived)

Dead organic matter
breaks down to form
humus.

Parent material, breaks
down by weathering
to form inorganic (mineral)
matter (pebbles,
sand, silt and clay)

Figure 8 A typical soil profile for lowland Britain

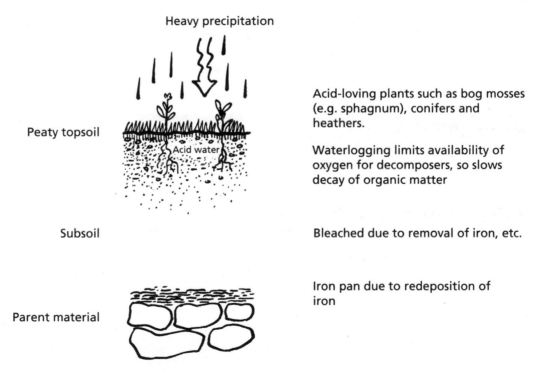

Heavy precipitation

Peaty topsoil

Acid water

Subsoil

Parent material

Acid-loving plants such as bog mosses
(e.g. sphagnum), conifers and
heathers.

Waterlogging limits availability of
oxygen for decomposers, so slows
decay of organic matter

Bleached due to removal of iron, etc.

Iron pan due to redeposition of
iron

Figure 9 A typical soil profile for a moorland in upland Britain

Note: boundaries are sharp because there are few worms to mix the layers due to the high acidity
of the soil.

Suggested activity: Is my soil acid?

Upland soils tend to be acid. Lowland and limestone/chalk tend to be less acid, or neutral. Children could investigate the acidity of the soil using red cabbage. Beforehand you need to take some very finely chopped fresh red (purple) cabbage, cooked in just enough water so that it is barely covered. The juice can then be mixed with the soil by the children. If the result is that the juice changes to red, then the soil is acidic. If it changes to blue/purple, it is alkaline.

TEACHER'S BACKGROUND PARTICLE SIZE IN SOILS

The size of soil particles has a notable effect on a soil's properties and uses. Children enjoy discovering these properties and diagnosing their usefulness by experimenting with making various shapes, as described in the activity on page 43.

Table 7 Soil properties and uses

	Sand KS 1	Silt KS 2	Clay KS 1	Loam KS 2	Peat KS 2
Size of particles	0.2 – 2mm	Not visible without magnification		Mixture of sand, silt and clay	Variable
Feel	Gritty	Silky	Sticky	Mixture of sand, silt and clay.	Fibrous or smooth. Light weight when dry.
Suitability for plant growth	Drains well but holds little plant food and moisture. Warms quickly.	Hold moisture and plant food but warms and drains slowly.		Has advantages of sand, silt and clay. The best soil for growing most plants.	Holds moisture well. Usually good but often short of nutrients.
Other properties	Easily blown by wind as grains are not cohesive when dry.				Partly rotted plant remains often visible. Dark brown/ black colour from dead organic matter.

Key: KS1 Suggested soil terminology for KS1
KS2 Suggested additional terminology for KS2

ACTIVITY: HOW TO FIND OUT WHAT TYPE OF SOIL YOU HAVE – TRY MAKING SOIL DOUGHNUTS!

Wet your soil sample, squeeze it out, then knead it and see which of the shapes in the table you can make, starting with A, then B then C and so on. When you cannot make the next one, look up the name of your soil in the table.

Table 8 Soil types

Shape	Code		Soil type
Cone	A	=	SAND
Ball	B	=	SANDY LOAM
Sausage	C	=	SILT LOAM
'Worm'	D	=	LOAM
'Horseshoe'	E	=	CLAY LOAM
'Tyre'	F	=	LIGHT CLAY
'Inner tube'	G	=	HEAVY CLAY

Teacher's demonstration: Another way of finding out what your soil contains

Suggested activity: Settling jar

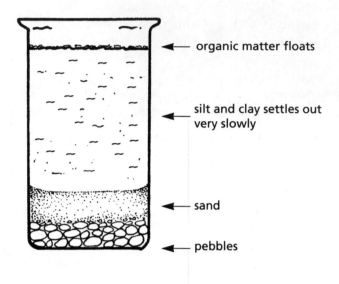

organic matter floats

silt and clay settles out very slowly

sand

pebbles

Take a tall jar, fill ¾ full with water and then decant. Add ¼ jar of soil, then the water. Notice that the jar is not full to the top: some water has filled the air spaces in the soil. Put the lid on and shake the jar well, then watch the grains settle into layers: the pebbles and sand will settle quickly, the silt and clay will settle out over the next day, whilst the organic matter will float. A series of jars can be used to illustrate differences between soils.

The 'Earthworm Song' and the following activity (see page 47) will help children to understand and enjoy the work of worms in the soil.

EARTHWORM

I am an earthworm and I'm a friend to you
I make little tunnels in the earth to let the air and water through
The soil is my dinner and tea and the soil is my home
And me and me cousins when we work together turn dirt into fertile loam
(Loam, that's when the soil is all soft and crumbly)

Now this is a bit embarrassing but I'll tell you 'cos you're my friend
All the leaves and soil I eat come out my other end
It's called worm castings and it's full of minerals and such
It's good for the plants, it helps them grow and they like it very much

I don't live very long, just one year or two
And so all my life I'm working hard to make good soil for you
So if you find me cover me up, don't leave me high and dry
'Cos the birds might eat me or in the hot summer I'll shrivel and die
(Well I'm off, gonna get a wriggle on, all this talk about birds
is makin' me nervous – see you later).

Earthworm

Words & music: Fay White

ACTIVITY: THE ROTTER'S RESTAURANT

Rotters or decomposers break down material from the bodies of animals and plants and release the goodness in them so that they can be used again.

Dig down in some soil covered with leaf litter. At the surface you will find whole leaves, and then bits of leaves. Soon you will not be able to recognise the leaves at all. This shows how rotters break down leaves and help make soil. Fungi, soil minibeasts and bacteria make excellent rotters.

MAKE SURE YOU ASK PERMISSION BEFORE YOU DIG YOUR HOLE, AND FILL IT UP AGAIN AFTERWARDS.

WASH YOUR HANDS.

ROTTER'S DELIGHT

The puzzle below shows what five rotters eat. Use the information to write an advert or menu for the Rotter's Restaurant.

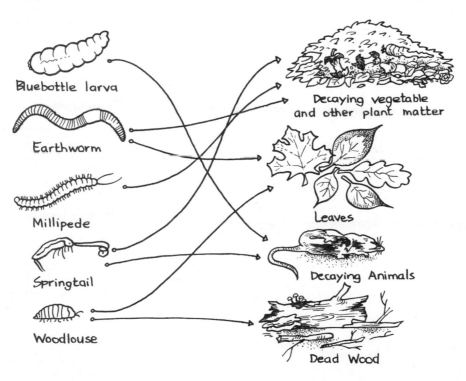

Why not use leaves, vegetable peelings, apple cores, grass clippings and egg shells to make your own compost heap – the perfect ROTTER'S RESTAURANT.

Reproduced from 'LINK' with permission of Wildlife Watch. (The Wildlife Trusts, The Green, Witham Park, Waterside South, Lincoln LN5 7JR. Tel: 01522 544400. Fax: 01522 511616.)

Some interesting facts about soil life

- The number of micro-organisms in one tablespoonful of soil may be more than the total number of people who have ever lived.

- Charles Darwin estimated that 25 tons of worm casts could be produced per hectare per year.

- The weight of worms under grassland may be more than the livestock grazing on top.

Teacher's Demonstration: A wormery

Pour warm water over a metre square patch of soil to encourage worms to rise to the surface. Then calculate how many worms would be found in a larger plot. Alternatively cover the soil with black polythene several days before you want to collect worms; the black material will absorb heat and draw worms towards the surface.

Set up a wormery in the classroom. This could be a tall thin, glass-sided box or fish tank. Fill with layers of different coloured soil and place leaf remains on the surface. Add worms and keep the soil moist. Keep covered from the light when not observing worms. Observe every three or four days.

ACTIVITY FOR THE AUTUMN:
A LEAF'S LIFE

Choose your favourite leaf from the school
grounds or park. Spend a little while
thinking about your leaf's life.
Which branch was it born on and when?
What helped it to grow?
Why and when did it die?
Now make it a little grave in the soil.
Do you know what happens to it next?
(As it rots the food in it will feed other
plants and animals.)
Do you know what we call it when
something is used again?
Draw some pictures in the box below to show
what happened to the leaf during
its life

COMPOST

All life on land begins and ends in the soil. The recycling process can be demonstrated by designing a school compost bin as explained on p.00. The 'Compost Makers' Work Song' will add interest here (see p. 51 overleaf).

At this stage, it is useful to introduce children to sustainable methods of gardening and farming. These make use of the principles of recycling through compost making, which is summarised in Figure 10 on p. 54.

Suggested activities

- Find out what is biodegradable: See Activity 1, Figure 11 on page 55.

- Construct a school compost heap and encourage children to recycle their lunch scraps by composting them. Figure 12 on page 56 gives practical advice on how to do this.

- Find out what happens inside a compost heap. See Activity 2, Figure 11 on page 55.

- Have children form themselves into research teams to survey the school community about their attitudes to composting.

- Conduct a publicity campaign in the local community to raise awareness about the value of compost.

THE COMPOST MAKERS' WORK SONG

We are compost makers, we make compost well
We know how to make it so it will not stink or smell
If you pay attention, you can make it too
Listen to our good advice and you'll know what to do

Chorus 1

Take foodscraps from the kitchen
To a suitable outside spot
And mix 'em up with old lawn clippings
And tea-leaves from the teapot
Apple cores, fallen leaves and next door's old dead cat
Some cow dung, chook poo*, horse manure
And Uncle Hedley's hat

Micro-organisms are living in the soil
They do all the decomposing work and all the toil
So add a couple of layers of good garden earth
And all those microbeasts will multiply for all they're worth

Chorus 2

Use your food scraps from the kitchen
In your suitable outside spot
Mix 'em up with old lawn clippings
And tea-leaves from the teapot
Apple cores, fallen leaves and next door's old dead cat
Some cow dung, chook poo*, horse manure
And Uncle Hedley's hat

Compost should be airy, damp but not too dry
So water it a little bit and turn it from time to time
Don't let it get soggy, or it will puke and pong
If it's on the bugle boys, you know you've done it wrong

So save your kitchen food scraps, don't put them in the bin
Develop a sense of humus, with your next of kin
Learn to work together, follow nature's way
Listen to our song and start your compost heap today

* chook poo – Australian for chicken manure

Compost Maker's Work Song

Steady march

Words & music: Fay White

Figure 10 Nature's cycle: children's background

What is organic gardening?

Organic means something that is or was once alive. Organic gardens are a part of nature, filled with lots of different plants and garden wildlife. Organic gardeners try to understand and work with nature to help the garden grow. They do not use chemical fertilisers to feed plants or use chemical sprays to kill pests.

The Sun helps plants to grow

The gardener eats a tomato

Animals feed the soil

The tomato leaves are composted

Plants feed animals

The gardener gives a carrot to the rabbit

The rabbit droppings are composted

Worms start to make the compost

Soil creatures turn the compost into plant food and humus

The compost is put on to the garden

Tomatoes

Carrots

Humus helps to build the soil, and plant food feeds the plants

Worms

The soil feeds plants

Fungi

Bacteria

Nature's cycle

Nature works in a cycle, everything helping everything else to grow. In a wood, trees use gases from the air, water and food from the soil, and energy from the sun to grow. In turn, they feed animals with leaves, nuts, and berries. Animal droppings, dead leaves and branches fall to the ground. When the animals and trees eventually die they too end up on the soil. All these things make up organic matter. Take a look at some woodland soil. It is full of little creatures and fungi, which eat the organic matter and turn it into plant food. Everything is recycled so that it can be used again, with no waste. Organic gardens work in cycles too. See if you can spot any cycles in your garden.

From 'Muck and Magic' by Jo Readman, illustrated by Polly Pinder, published by Search Press, 1993. This version redrawn by Martin Cater.

Figure 11 Compost making

ANIMALS and plants which have died are recycled in the soil. Some things decay or degrade more quickly than others and certain conditions help this to happen. Compost heaps help the decay and recycling to happen quickly. Compost is so full of active living things that it gets hot while it is working. Finished compost is a very good fertiliser for plants.

ACTIVITY: WHAT IS BIODEGRADABLE?

Make a collection of different things and discuss how degradable they are. Test these predictions by burying the things in soil and then checking them every week or so. A good collection can be made by asking children to collect all the packaging and leftovers from supper one evening, or to collect litter (including nature's litter!) from the playground.

Discuss what conditions help things to degrade and the use of different packaging materials compared to nature's packaging materials like banana skins and pea pods.

ACTIVITY: INSIDE A COMPOST HEAP

Compost takes from six weeks to six months before it is ready to use. It is home to many different kinds of creatures who help in the process of decay. The class can be involved in this real life drama.

Make a set of cards with different colours representing the four main groups of compost organisms: fungus (10–60°C); cool-loving bacteria (10–50°C); heat-loving bacteria (40–70°C) and mini-beasts (10–30°C). On each write down the minimum and maximum temperature the organisms can work at, varying each slightly, and then add some other information about that organism, for example, what it eats or how it might move.

Mark out a 'compost heap' in the classroom – you might use tables on their sides. On the board write up a timeline, divided into weeks from 1 to 12. Write up the temperature in a week and let the 'organisms' decide if they can live in the heap. While there, they can move about doing what that organism does, until the next week's temperature is announced. Afterwards the class can discuss what was happening.

Week	1	2	3	4	5	6	7	8	9	10	11	12
Temp	15°C	30°C	50°C	60°C	70°C	70°C	60°C	50°C	40°C	30°C	20°C	15°C

FUNGUS (10–60°)

COOL-LOVING BACTERIA (10–50°)

HEAT-LOVING BACTERIA (40–70°)

MINI BEASTS (10–30°)

MAIN IDEAS

- Living things are recycled by the process of decay.
- Temperature, moisture, air and microbes are important for decay.
- Rates of decay vary.
- Compost recycles waste produce into useful fertiliser.

Reproduced with permission from 'Food, Farms and Futures' produced by the Soil Association. For their address, see p. 87.

Figure 12 Making a compost heap

ACTIVITY: MAKING A COMPOST HEAP

A good compost heap should be easy to fill, keep rain off the compost, let air circulate, keep heat in and be easy to empty when ready. Divide the class into groups and set them the task of designing and building a compost heap. They should be given a list of requirements and materials they could use.

MAKING A COMPOST HEAP

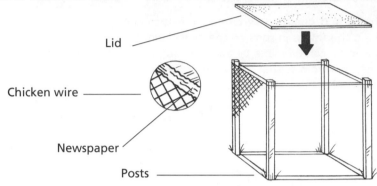

Lid

Chicken wire

Newspaper

Posts

RECORDING:
■ Make pictures of what happens inside a compost heap.
■ Graphs of temperature or rate of decomposition.
■ Computer spreadsheet or database of temperatures in a heap over time.
■ Make models of designs for compost heaps.
■ Write descriptive stories about what happens in a compost heap.

WATCH OUT FOR . . .
■ Comments about decay and change.
■ The uses of compost to condition soil and as a source of plant nutrients.
■ Discussion of temperature, moisture or air as necessary for decay.
■ The idea of cycles of nutrients.

EXTENSION IDEAS:
■ Make a collection of the mini-beasts found in compost.
■ Stopping decay by preserving using drying, freezing, vacuums, pickles, sugar.
■ Setting up a school composting and recycling unit.
■ Using microscopes and hand lenses to look at compost more closely.

EQUIPMENT

Thermometers (digital), coloured cards, some rubbish or litter, cardboard, chicken wire, wooden posts, newspaper, scrap wood.

SITE

Playground, school garden.

COMMENTS

Litter from a playground will be cleaner than from a bin. These activities are best followed over time to show how things change. Remember to wash hands and use gloves.

ORGANIC DECAY

An organic farm or garden tries to work as a 'closed system', with few external inputs. To do this successfully, great care must be taken to make the best use of everything produced and to return to the soil as much as possible of what has been removed. One of the best ways is to make compost of the plant material and animal waste which is produced by growing crops or rearing animals.

On a farm the compost heaps may be very big, sometimes in rows up to 50 metres long and 3 metres wide. Compost can be spread on the land using machines. Making compost means organic farms don't have to use synthetic fertilisers.

Reproduced with permission from 'Food, Farms and Futures' produced by the Soil Association.
For their address, see p. 87.

TEACHER'S BACKGROUND WHY IS SOIL IMPORTANT?

Soil is important in order to grow plants, upon which we all depend directly or indirectly for our food. Children could investigate how different land uses are often related to different soil types.

Table 9 The relationship between soil types and land uses

Activity	Soil type	Reason
Dairy farming	clayey	holds moisture so grows lush grass
Golf course or race course	sandy	drains well (is permeable) so fit to use after wet weather
Market gardening	loam or peat	fertile and easy to work, especially early in the growing season
Sheep farming	infertile soil	the small breeds of sheep can best survive the harsh conditions of hills and mountains where infertile soils are found.

NB These are generalisations: there are many other factors which affect land use such as tradition, access to market, technology, climate, economic and political factors.

The song on page 58 enables children to make the link between soil and economic activity. 'Land Links' is most suitable for KS1.

TEACHER'S BACKGROUND WHAT'S HAPPENING TO OUR SOILS?

Threats to our soil

You should be able to demonstrate clearly to children that the way in which we manage soil is usually very unsustainable. Thus they should be able to understand the need to take care of this resource, something that they can practise in the school grounds or their own gardens.

Threats to our soil are illustrated in Figure 13 on page 62. One of the most worrying is soil erosion. It's estimated that the average soil loss per annum per hectare is over 3 tonnes, which is much faster than the rate at which soil is being formed. Even in areas where soil forms very fast the rate is only 2 tonnes per annum, and in Britain it is only 0.2 – 0.5 tonnes. What's more, it's also believed that over one-third of the world's arable land is at risk of becoming desert. Soil is then another non-renewable resource.

These problems are not restricted to poverty-stricken areas of the tropics: there are serious problems here in Britain, where 44 per cent of our arable land is estimated to be at risk. Soil loss of 200 tonnes per hectare per year has been recorded on the Sussex Downs.

LAND LINKS

What am I wearing? You're wearing a jumper
What is it made of? It's made of wool
Where does wool grow? It grows on a sheep
And to grow that wool a sheep has to eat
And a sheep eats the good green grass
And the grass grows on the land

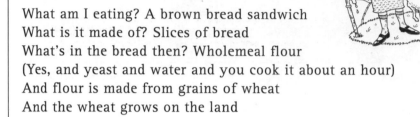

What am I eating? A brown bread sandwich
What is it made of? Slices of bread
What's in the bread then? Wholemeal flour
(Yes, and yeast and water and you cook it about an hour)
And flour is made from grains of wheat
And the wheat grows on the land

Chorus
Lots of things around me
Things I can see or touch with my hand
Most of the things I have or need
Are linked somehow to the land

What am I drinking? Fresh squeezed orange juice
What is it made of? Oranges of course!
And where does an orange grow? Now let me see
An orange has to grow on an orange tree!
And an orange tree's roots are deep in the soil
And the soil is part of the land

What am I drinking? Cool clear water
Where did it come from? Out of the tap
What's the tap joined to? A pipe underground
Which goes to a big dam a long way from town
And the dam is filled from rivers all round
And the rivers flow through the land

Chorus
Now it's your turn. Yes now it's your turn
Find out where these things come from
Glass and paper, eggs and cheese
Chocolate cake, fizzy drink, honey and bees
Book and pencils and bicycle wheels – find out
Which ones come from the land

It may surprise you – it may surprise you . . .

Landlinks

Medium Swing   Words & music: Fay White

1. What am I wearing? You're wearing a jumper — What is it made of? It's made of wool — Where does wool grow? It grows on a sheep — and to grow that wool a sheep has to eat, & a sheep, eats, the good green grass & the grass grows on the land —

... It may surprise you—

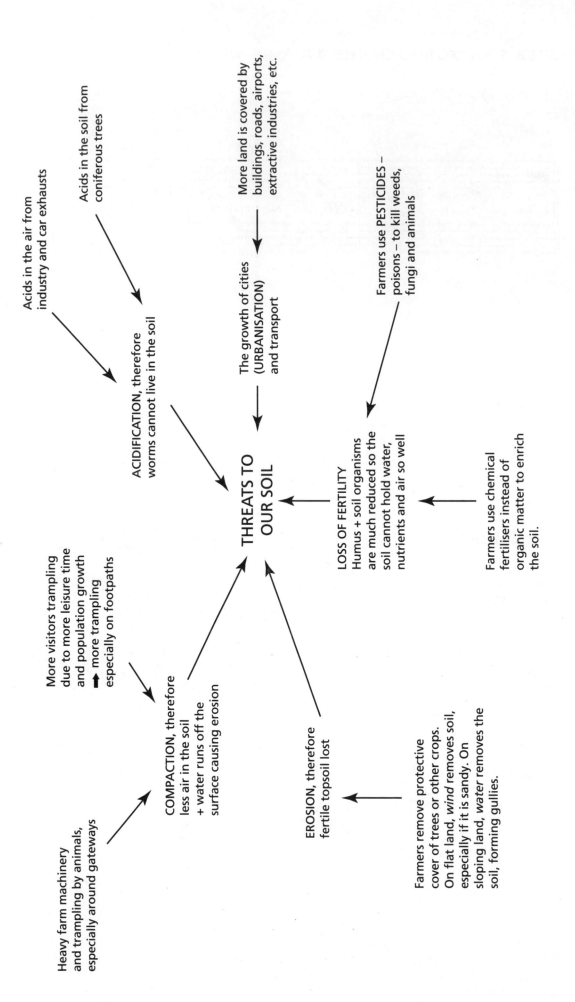

Figure 13 Threats to our soil: teachers' background

TEACHER'S BACKGROUND THE WEARING WIND

Wind wears away, or ERODES, the soil.

Activity	Teacher's notes
What you'll need: 1. 2 sheets of board approx. 30 × 30cm and 60 × 30cm. Set up as shown, with a support behind the vertical board. 2. 2cm of fine, dry, sandy soil. 3. A variable-speed hair drier. 	Bricks will form suitable supports. A rectangular cardboard 'fan' can be used instead of a hair drier.
What to do: Turn the hair drier on full and see what happens. Now reduce the speed and see what happens. Now try different types of soil: clay and peat, both wet and dry.	Larger particles and more soil moved at faster speeds.
What did you learn? What happened 1 at high wind speeds, 2 at low wind speeds?	Dry soil is most easily moved because moisture makes particles cohesive. Dry peat is the easiest to move (plant matter: this can be demonstrated using the settling jar experiment on p. 44).
What type of soil is most easily carried away (eroded) by the wind? 1 wet/dry? 2 sand/clay/peat?	Dry sand is easier to move than dry clay because sand particles are not cohesive like clay.
Which layer of the soil is worn away? Which layer has most plant food in it?	Topsoil which contains most nutrients is worn away.
Where and when do we see bare soil which could be worn away by the wind?	Bare soil occurs on arable land after ploughing from autumn to spring in Britain, in drier climates where few plants can grow, on trampled areas or where overgrazing occurs.
Do you think wind will be as much a problem in hilly areas?	Wind erosion is a greater problem on level plains, e.g. the Dust Bowl in the USA, or the Fens and East Anglia in Britain. Hills provide some shelter though wind speeds may be high when funnelled up a valley.

The cartoons in Figure 14 on pages 65–70 are useful for consolidating the concept of the importance of vegetation for binding soil as well as explaining soil formation in sand dunes.

Teachers' questions	Children's answers
Look at cartoon 3	
Which way is the wind blowing?	From left to right.
How can you tell?	The wind has bent the grass.
What is the name of the plant which holds the sand down?	Marram grass.
How do you think this plant holds the sand down?	Its roots bind the sand and its leaves give shelter so the wind is not powerful enough to carry the sand away.

Figure 14 The Story of Mr Marram and Mr Sand: Children's Background

Cartoons taken from 'The Great Aeolian Dune Story, featuring Mr Sand' originally produced in 1981 by Parks Canada, Prince Edward Island National Park. Original design by Lee Sackett, illustrations by Michael Fog, and text by Jerry L'Orange with technical expertise from Paul DeMone and Philip Michael. Printed by permission from the Department of Canadian Heritage, Prince Edward Island. This version redrawn by Martin Cater.

These small piles eventually grow into larger dunes. Often they are moved by the wind.

Eventually some plants begin to grow in the sand. Marram grass is the main plant. This plant holds the sand grains together. It helps to stop the dunes being blown away.

After a time other types of plants start to grow in the dunes, as soil begins to form. Then insects and other animals arrive.

Trampling over sand dunes can often kill marram grass. If the marram grass dies there is nothing to hold the sand together. The dunes blow away and the plants and animals no longer have anywhere to live.

On slopes, water can flow fast enough to pick up and carry away (erode) soil particles. The activity on page 73 shows how you can demonstrate soil erosion by helping the children to build model 'valleys'. Note that the activity requires you to provide a **mulch** – a material which is spread over the soil surface to reduce weed, growth and evaporation. The experiment could also be set up with two extra cartons at different inclines to test the effect of slope angle on erosion rates. Other variations include erecting 'hedges' across the slope and creating furrows either down or across the slope to illustrate the beneficial effects of hedgerows and **contour ploughing** (i.e. furrows across the slope). (See Figure 15 below) Also, introduce the term **catchment** to the children before working on the activity. This means the area from which water drains into a river. A good analogy is a roof draining into a gutter.

Farming practices which *cause* soil erosion by water

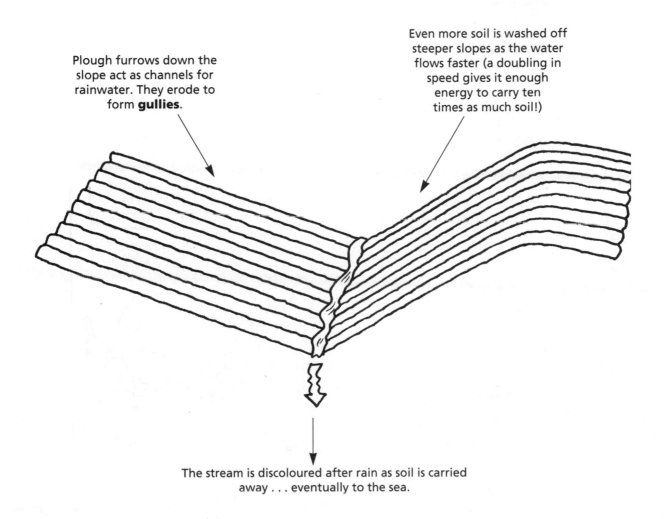

Plough furrows down the slope act as channels for rainwater. They erode to form **gullies**.

Even more soil is washed off steeper slopes as the water flows faster (a doubling in speed gives it enough energy to carry ten times as much soil!)

The stream is discoloured after rain as soil is carried away . . . eventually to the sea.

Figure 15 Farming practices affecting soil erosion by water

Farming practices which help to *reduce* soil erosion by water

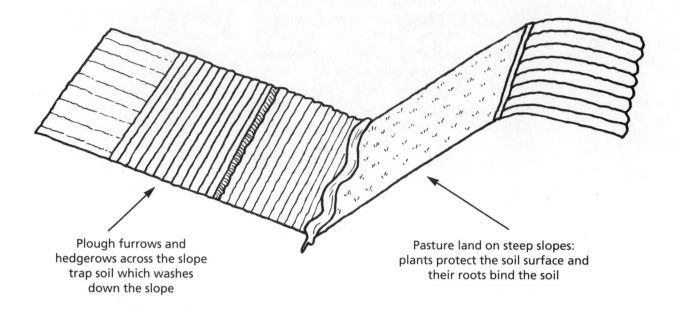

Plough furrows and
hedgerows across the slope
trap soil which washes
down the slope

Pasture land on steep slopes:
plants protect the soil surface and
their roots bind the soil

ACTIVITY: THE WICKED WATER

When rain falls on soil, the soil soaks it up like a sponge. However, in heavy rain not all water can be absorbed so some water will run down slopes and wash soil away. In this experiment you will make two different valleys to see how running water causes soil erosion. In one valley you will have a protective cover (a mulch) on the soil; in the other, you will have bare soil.

What you'll need:

- 2 rulers or a measuring jug

- 2 waxed cartons (1, or preferably, 2 litre size)

- scissors

- soil

- mulch material (such as grass clippings, etc) shallow containers

- watering can or 'clouds' (made from a plastic bottle with a cloud motif cut from a piece of white paper and stuck onto it) and with holes drilled into the bottle top.

What to do:

1. With the pouring side face up, prepare the cartons by cutting out the section marked in the diagram.

open the carton on one side and cut away the top.

sealed flap on top of carton

2. Fill the cartons to the lip with soil.

what you finish with!

3. Place a layer of mulch material over the soil in one of the cartons.
4. Tip the two cartons to represent a slope. Gently pour a measured quantity of water from the watering can on to the top end. Put the shallow containers at the bottom end. Hold a ruler in each so that you can measure how much water enters (or use a measuring jug).

Now you can see how the two different valleys behave. How will you make it a fair test?

Sprinkle the same amount of water over each catchment and measure the time it takes for the water to flow into the container at the base.

Measure the amount of water in the containers.

	Mulched valley	Unmulched valley
Water at start		
Water at finish		
Time taken		
In which catchment is the soil more likely to wear away?		

TEACHERS' BACKGROUND THE SOIL SQUASHERS

Heavy machinery and trampling by people and animals pound and compact the soil. All plants and animals living on or in the soil are likely to be squashed. Also, some plants may be unable to re-establish themselves if the ground is too hard. The activity on page 75 demonstrates very clearly the effects of trampling on the variety of life in soil.

ACTIVITY: THE SOIL SQUASHERS

What you'll need:

- 2 suspended light bulbs
- 2 large colanders with fine holes
- 2 pieces of white paper
- hand trowel
- enough soil to fill the colanders

What to do:

As early as possible in the day look for areas in your school grounds where people have worn away the grass and compacted the soil. Take a sample of topsoil. Next, look for a sample of soil from a bed (where soil has not been compacted). Fill the colanders and rest them on a piece of white paper.

Suspend a bulb above to dry the soil slowly, so causing the animals to move down on to the white paper.

Check regularly to see how many have come out of each soil.

What you saw:

Count the number and types of animals that fall out of each soil sample and write your answers here:

NB Put all animals back where you found them as soon as possible!

What you learned:

Which sample had the most soil animals in it? Why do you think this is?

MUD IN OUR SCHOOL

The following case study, Mud in our School, is reproduced with permission from the Curriculum Council for Wales, 1993, 'An Enquiry Approach to Learning Geography'. It is a very good example of a broader and longer investigation into soil erosion.

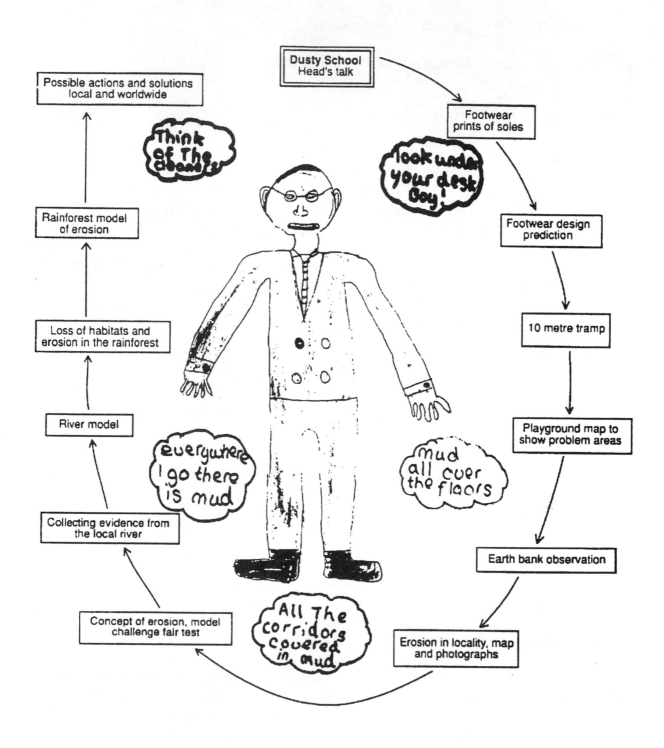

Focus

For some time staff and governors of our school had been concerned about the build-up of dust and mud in the building, especially during wet weather. This concern was seen as an opportunity to give a topical slant to an enquiry into the work of rivers and the effects of rainfall on the landscape. The enquiry was part of a unit of work on buildings and habitats which would include a study of erosion and destruction of habitats in the rainforests.

Stimulus and structure

A suitably stimulating and thought-provoking start for the enquiry was needed, and the headteacher was asked to visit the classroom to 'voice his concerns' about the problem of mud in the school.

While a clear route through the enquiry had been planned, opportunities were provided for children to suggest ways of approaching specific questions. Teachers know that clearly-structured questions lead children down pre-planned avenues of enquiry. Class discussions lead to children offering a variety of ideas which can be sifted and selected by the class in the light of practicability, availability of resources and relevance to both the enquiry and the overall project in hand.

The 'mud factor'

During the headteacher's mock tirade, the children glanced at the door and their footwear, and the discussion that followed his departure threw up the suggestion that some children were transporting more mud than others because of the design of the soles of their shoes. A printing workshop was set up to record the patterns of the soles. When the prints could be handled, ridges and dips in the rubber soles were identified and the shoes labelled by groups of children with a 'mud factor' of 1 to 9, smooth soles being allocated a factor of 1 due to their inability to carry much mud into school.

As back-up for our observations that smoother soles picked up less mud, a '10-metre tramp' was devised. Each design of shoe was walked through a course of damp, shallow earth and then dropped five times into a tray so that mud being transported on the sole could be weighed and the results compared with our estimated 'mud factors'.

Sources of mud

The next step was to identify sources of mud in the school grounds, and in groups the children marked on large-scale maps the areas they thought were causing the problem. In addition to well-worn short-cuts, they noted a

SOILS   77

sloping bank alongside the playground where the grass had been worn away and the soil was being washed on to the playing surface in wet weather.

The effects of water and gravity acting together on a surface were explored through open-ended questioning and one child even offered the word 'erosion'.

Erosion

This knowledge could now be applied to other situations, and local maps and oblique photographs were studied to locate slopes and possible evidence of erosion. One aerial photograph of a coal tip with its deep V-shaped gulley formations illustrated this particularly well.

The discussion progressed to angle of slope, speed of run-off and amounts of material that could be dislodged and transported. The children were challenged to build a model to illustrate the effects of different angles of slope on the speed of water. Brainstorming produced some wondrous schemes, but the favoured design utilised a length of plastic gutter, stacking chairs to lift one end to different heights, a plastic container to collect eroded material and a watering can to simulate a rainstorm.

A dual assessment was possible here when the analysis of data collected and the operation of the fair test were taken into account.

A visit to the local river allowed pupils to observe evidence of erosion, transport and deposition in the field.

The river model

The pupils were now challenged to design and build, through collaborative effort, a model to illustrate all they had learned so far about the work of a river. Groups buzzed and sketches appeared, from which details and ideas were amalgamated to form the 'class' design for the model. Three wooden boards and a metal tray were set up to represent the course of a river from the top of a mountain to the sea.

Sand was spread out and the tray filled with water. A watering can provided the rainfall in the hills and the children were delighted to find that erosion began at once. During refills children were asked to point out features they recognised. Cocktail sticks with numbered flags were stuck in the sand to mark features using terms like bedrock, most erosion, valley, undercutting, tributary, island and delta. The school video camera was used so that children could take the film home to show parents the kind of work they were involved in.

Note: If you are short of time, then the Wicked Water activity on page 73 could be used.

The rainforests

The concept of erosion had been traced from classroom to playground, on to the local river and to a model of any river. Our attention now turned to the wider world. Loss of habitats in the rainforests, pictures of virgin forests, loggers at work, burning of tree remains, smoke clouds over the Amazon Basin and cattle struggling to graze on what was left brought to light not only the plight of the local people but also the speed of destruction.

The connection between our earlier work and the problems of the rainforest was made when two garden trays of soil were tilted on bricks. In one, cress had been grown to represent, in miniature, the lush growth of the rainforest. The tray containing bare soil was to be the forest after cutting and burning. The watering-can rainstorm this time gave spectacular results. The clinging roots of the cress held the soil very well while the land devoid of 'trees' lost much of its soil to the torrent of water.

Action and solutions

It is easy to imagine how enquiries like this can set up worries in children's minds, so the final phase of this type of work should always focus on action that can be taken and potential solutions to the problems posed within the issue. Attitudes may need to be changed. Children completed surveys for homework, to be done with parents, into the amounts of hardwood and softwood used in their homes. The 'mahogany detectives' enjoyed reprimanding parents about their over-indulgence in tropical forest products. Letters were written to Parliament to let ministers know of their concern for the 'lungs of the world'.

The children concluded the exercise with a list of suggestions to solve the problem in our school: the bank of earth causing the problem for our school should be re-seeded and children kept off it; better doormats should be provided and indoor shoes considered.

Table 10 Mud in our school

Focus for enquiry: mud in our school (or what are the effects of erosion?)		
Key stage: 2 Year: 6 Time allocated: 2 weeks		
Key questions	**Knowledge, understanding, skills, values and attitudes**	**Teaching/learning activities**
Why is there mud in our school?	Identify the method of transporting material from playground and surrounding area	Brainstorm possible cause; estimate and test the effect of different designs of soles
Where is the mud coming from?	Use map to locate features outside the classroom	Walk around site with a map marking muddy areas
How can we show what happens when rain falls on different slopes?	The effects of different surfaces on rainwater when it reaches the ground	Develop a fair test to show effect of different slopes on rainfall
Where else might we find evidence of erosion in our local area?	Compare oblique and vertical air photographs with maps to locate possible sites and 'interpret' relief maps	Look for slopes, streams and contours on maps and photographs
What evidence is there that rivers erode?	Identify parts of a river system; identify evidence that rivers erode, transport and deposit material; draw a sketch map	Build a model of a river from source to mouth, simulate the effect of water flow; observe the features of a river; visit local river and observe evidence; draw a sketch map of site
What is the effect of erosion in the rainforest?	Investigate effects on the environment of extracting natural resources	Locate the Amazon on a map; study photographs of tree-felling, burning of wood, clouds of smoke over the rainforest, soil erosion and resulting poor grazing land; compare the effect of rain on tray of cress and tray of bare soil
What could we do about the problems of mud in our school and erosion in the rainforest?	Understand that action can be taken to slow down/stop the damage and repair it; raise awareness of people's values and attitudes towards problems	Homework: compile list of things made in your home from soft and hardwood; why should people buy fewer rainforest products?; problem-solving suggestions at our sites in the school grounds

Table 11 Cross-curricular focus: environmental education

Resources needed	Assessment opportunities	Time
Sheet of glass, printing ink, rubber roller		3 hours
Maps of grounds	Children mark features on a large-scale map	1 hour
Tray, plastic guttering, watering can and soil	Carrying out test, observing and analysing data	1 day for all groups to try the test chosen after brainstorming of children's ideas
Maps and photographs of local area	Children describe to teacher the link between contours on map and slope seen on photographs	2 hours
Sand, wooden boards, large metal tray, watering can; map of local river	Children identify parts of a river system including sources, channel, tributaries and mouth; selecting stones from numbered set to answer questions in a quiz designed to highlight processes of erosion and deposition, e.g. which stone do you think has travelled furthest downstream?	½ day to build and another day for groups to use the simulation; 1 hour on site plus ½ hour for quiz
Variety of photographs from magazines and textbooks; 1 seed tray containing soil; 1 seed tray containing cress; watering can	Write a letter to the Brazilian Embassy explaining concern over erosion	1½ hours
Help of parent	Mark rainforests on world map; explain why some environments need special protection; describe an activity designed to improve the local environment; suggest ways of restoring damaged landscapes	1 hour

HOW MIGHT YOU END THE TOPIC?

The following pages (83–86) give examples of activities which you can photocopy for use in end-of-unit assessments.

Teacher's background for the activities

In the first activity, shown on page 83, the samples used were clayey and sandy soils. If you don't have access to these types, a substitute can be made by mixing clay or sand, respectively, with ordinary garden topsoil. Subsoil should be taken from about 60cm depth.

The objects that were made available for the activity were: funnels, filter papers (Jey cloths are a useful substitute), margarine tubs, measuring jugs, bricks, gravel trays and newspaper.

In the second activity, shown on page 84, the 'shaking' experiment referred to is the settling jar activity on page 44.

Suitable answers for the 'What can we do to help?' section in the third activity (page 85) might be:

1. Plant more trees.

2. Keep the soil covered by crops for as long as possible.

3. Only use heavy machinery when the soil is dry (it's stronger then).

4. Get our energy from clean sources such as the sun, the wind and the waves.

5. Use safe ways of controlling pests such as introducing animals which eat the pests.

ACTIVITY: SOLVING SOIL MYSTERIES I
– PRACTICAL WORK

Here are some samples taken from my garden. See if you can answer the questions below. You can design your own experiments to help you solve the mysteries. You may use any of the objects set out on the table for your experiments.

1. Which soil do you think is the best to grow seeds in? Why? Remember what seeds need to grow.

2. In some parts of my garden, slugs are common. They love eating my cabbages and many other plants! Slugs like damp soil. Which soil holds the moisture best?

3. One way of keeping slugs away is to find a material which they do not like crawling over. This material can then be spread in a narrow band around the edge of the garden to keep slugs away. Which material do you think I used and why?

4. Which soil do you think is hardest to dig? Why?

5. The sample labelled subsoil is taken from 60cm below the surface: do you know why it is called subsoil? What happens when water reaches this layer?

6. My garden is on a slope. When it rains heavily, soil is worn away (we call this **erosion**). Which soil do you think suffers erosion most easily? Why?

7. Do you know what the soil is like

   (a) on the school sports field?

   (b) on your local recreation ground?

   (c) in your garden?

   You might like to collect samples and compare them.

Divide your page into two columns with the titles 'sandy soil' and 'clayey soil'. Answer in full sentences.

1. **Which soil**

   ● holds the moisture best?

   ● encourages slugs? (Remember they like the damp!)

   ● is unpleasant for slugs to crawl on so can be used as a barrier to keep them away from precious plants?

   ● is sticky to handle when wet so its grains hold together well and are not easily eroded (worn away)?

   ● is easily worn away (eroded) by water?

2. **Our soil pit**

You will remember digging a hole to find out what's underground. Draw a diagram, with measurements, of our pit. Use 'soil paints' or pieces of soil glued to your paper or card to show the different layers. Label with answers to the following questions.

(a) Which is the darkest layer? Describe the colours of all layers.

(b) When we did the 'shaking' experiment what did we find floating to the surface from this layer?

(c) Which layer breaks up into crumbs which would be good to grow seedlings in?

(d) Where did we find stones in the soil? Why?

(e) Where do most of the earthworms live? Why?

(f) Which part of the soil is hardest to dig?

(g) Which part of the soil is wettest? Why?

(h) How deep do roots of the plants go?

ACTIVITY:
PLANNING FOR THE FUTURE

What someone does today may be the cause of something which will happen in the future.

To learn how to care for the Earth we need to understand causes and effects.

See if you can match the causes and effects in the two lists by drawing an arrow between them.

What is happening today (causes)	What will happen in the future (effects)
Forests are cut down on steep slopes.	Wind carries away the soil.
Sandy soil on level land is left bare.	Wild animals may be killed.
Farmer uses poisons to kill pests on his crops.	Water cannot flow into the soil, so it flows off the surface and wears it away.
Power stations release gases which form acids in air.	Soil is washed off the slope into the river after a storm.
Heavy machinery compacts the soil.	Soil, rivers and lakes become acid, so worms and fish die.

What can we do to help?

Write what you think below.

ACTIVITY: THE SOIL DOCTOR – SOS: SAVE OUR SOILS!

Imagine that you are a doctor who cares for sick soils. Here is a list of soil problems.

Can you suggest some answers?

1   Water runs straight through the soil, so it's very dry.

2   The wind blows the soil away easily.

3   Water washes the soil down a slope.

4   The soil is spoilt along a path.

5   The soil does not have enough food in it and the farmer can't afford to buy fertiliser.
     (Clue: could he make his own?)

TEACHING SOILS IN THE CONTEXT OF PLACE STUDIES: AN EXEMPLAR

The table below gives an example of how you can use the topic soils as part of a scheme of work on place studies, at Key Stages 1 and 2. Most schools will be located in densely populated areas more likely to be on fertile lowland soils. However, columns one and two in Table 12 might need to be transposed for other schools. At KS2 the soil should be tied in with study of economic activity.

Table 12 Teaching soils at KS1 and 2

	Local area	Contrasting UK locality or EDC locality	
KS 1	Fertile soil of school grounds	An infertile (acid) soil of an upland area	Soil erosion is more marked in many EDC localities
	Wider local area	**Contrasting UK locality**	**EDC locality**
KS 2	Fertile soil used for dairy or arable farming or market gardening	Infertile soil used for sheep farming, reservoirs and conifer plantations	Concentration on a single crop for export often exhausts soils

RECOMMENDED TEACHING RESOURCES

1. *Food, Farming and Futures* for KS 2 and produced by the Soil Association, Bristol House, Victoria Street, Bristol BS1 6DF. (Tel: 01179 290661.) The Association has established a national network of organic farms open to the public, can set up school links and provide a comprehensive educational information service, including a free information pack in return for an A4 self-addressed envelope and first-class stamp.
2. *Muck and Magic* by Jo Readman, Search Press, 1993, colourful and informative, winner of an award for the best conservation book for 8–13 year-olds. Gives plenty of inspiration for children to start their own organic garden. (KS 2/3) £4.95.
3. *Landcare for Kids* produced in Australia, $10 + p & p from the Bookshop, Conservation, Forests and Lands Dept., 240 Victoria Road, E. Melbourne, Victoria 3002, Australia (KS 1 / KS 2). The tape includes several songs that are also reproduced on the CD-ROM which accompanies this pack: 'Soil Ain't Dirt', 'Earthworm', 'Land Links', and 'The Compost Makers' Work Song'.
4. *Grow Your Own: be an organic farmer*, by Thompson Yardley, 1993, London: Cassell (KS2).
5. Nuffield Science *Rocks, Soils and Weather*, 1993, London: Collins (KS2).
6. *Soil and Sky*, by Sue Dale Tunnicliffe, 1991, Blackwell Infant Science Series. Well-designed workcards (KS1).
7. *Growing Naturally – a teachers' guide to organic gardening* by Maggi Brown, 1997, HDRA. A practical guide. £8.99.

PART 3

Rocks

TEACHERS' BACKGROUND AND THE NEXT LAYER DOWN – ROCKS

It is logical to progress from soils to greater depths to the more solid part of the earth's crust. Unfortunately these materials are usually too hard for children to dig themselves, so we must rely on natural or man-made exposures.

Why study rocks?

Children find rocks fascinating both because of the mystery that they hold and their beauty: they fire the imagination, particularly if they contain fossils or crystals. This gives us an opportunity to help children understand our dependency on non-renewable rock resources such as coal, gas, oil, metals and many others. Rocks form a very useful link between NC Science and Geography.

Where should children experience rocks?

Ideally, children should experience rocks in the field. If you don't have suitable sites nearby, why not make a rock wall or a rock garden from a variety of large and attractive specimens or set medium-sized specimens in concrete on trays to use in the classroom? (For ease of transport you could fix castors to the base.) You could even, if you're feeling most adventurous, build a rock village! To do this you could use plaster of paris or Plasticine with pieces of sand, gravel or rock pressed on to give texture on walls and slates as roofing material.

Where to find specimens

It is not difficult to find specimens to study. Graveyards, and town centre shop fronts are a rich resource, the former safer to study. Off-cuts can be obtained from monumental masons. Specimens can be loaned from museums or secondary schools, or children can be asked to bring specimens into school (pebbles collected on beach holidays are particularly useful).

A suggested geological collection

The best choice for each school will vary:

Choose materials of local interest. A variety of colours, hardnesses and textures will stimulate the children's senses. Another criterion for choice of samples below was their economic value in preparation for learning about mining and quarrying.

1. Sedimentary rocks: sandstone, coal, limestone, mudstone.

2. Metamorphic rocks: marble and slate (the altered equivalents of limestone and mudstone respectively).

3. Igneous rocks: granite, basalt (or other fine-grained lava), pumice.

4. Minerals: quartz, gypsum, halite (rock salt) and a metallic mineral, e.g. pyrite (fool's gold).

5. Fossils: plant, animal (e.g. ammonite).

How rocks form

Having introduced the water cycle, the idea of the rock cycle might be introduced to year 6 or 7, though the enormous time taken for it to be completed (hundreds of millions of years) is hard to grasp. The various stages and processes in the cycle are illustrated in the inner circle of Figure 16 on p. 93. In the outer circle analogies and simpler words to explain the processes are given, which will help the children to understand the concepts more clearly.

Suggested activity: Fossil Flick Book

One aspect of rock formation which fascinates children is the process of fossilisation. Moreover, this explains the process of sedimentary rock formation. A very effective means of putting over the sequence of events is a flick book (see Figure 17). Reproduced with permission, from *Exploring Earth Science*, C. Creary *et al.* (1992), Northamptonshire County Council (for address details see p. 125).

TEACHER'S BACKGROUND WHAT ARE ROCKS?

Children can explore their understanding of the term 'rocks' through discussion, using specimens of living and non-living material, of varying densities, hardness and age. This will help them to appreciate that rocks are materials which are non-living (though may contain, of course, remains of once living organisms), relatively dense, hard and old. A specimen containing an extinct fossil (e.g. an ammonite or trilobite or even a dinosaur!) will help to clarify the age and 'no longer alive' concept.

Safety Note: Beware! The broken edges of rocks and minerals may be sharp. That's why Stone Age man used them as tools. Handle all rocks and minerals with care to avoid accidents and never break up specimens with a hammer unless you use a special geological hammer and protective goggles.

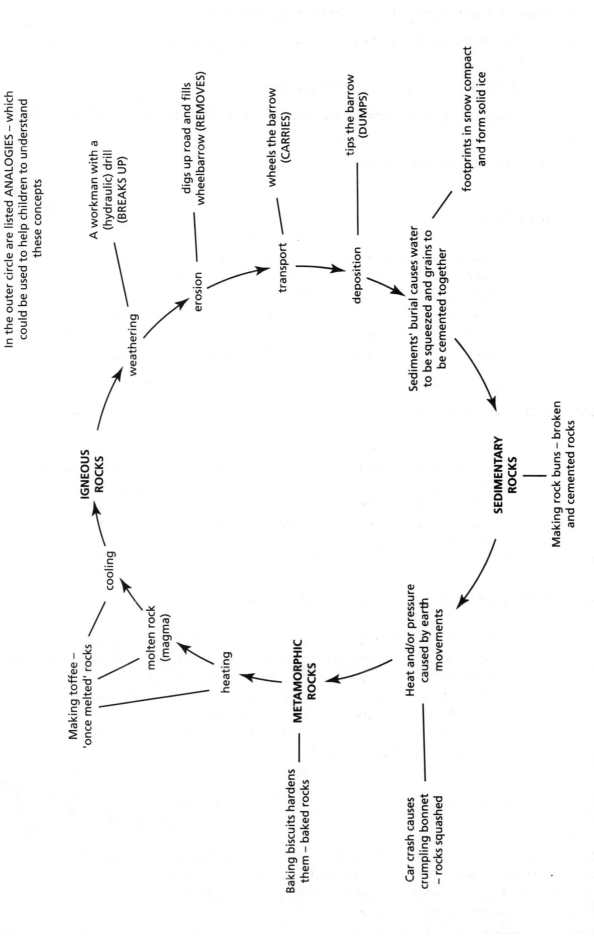

In the outer circle are listed ANALOGIES – which could be used to help children to understand these concepts

A workman with a (hydraulic) drill (BREAKS UP)

digs up road and fills wheelbarrow (REMOVES)

wheels the barrow (CARRIES)

tips the barrow (DUMPS)

footprints in snow compact and form solid ice

weathering

erosion

transport

deposition

Sediments' burial causes water to be squeezed and grains to be cemented together

IGNEOUS ROCKS

SEDIMENTARY ROCKS

Making rock buns – broken and cemented rocks

cooling

molten rock (magma)

heating

METAMORPHIC ROCKS

Heat and/or pressure caused by earth movements

Making toffee – 'once melted' rocks

Baking biscuits hardens them – baked rocks

Car crash causes crumpling bonnet – rocks squashed

Figure 16 The rock cycle: teacher's background and some simple ways of getting the concepts over to children

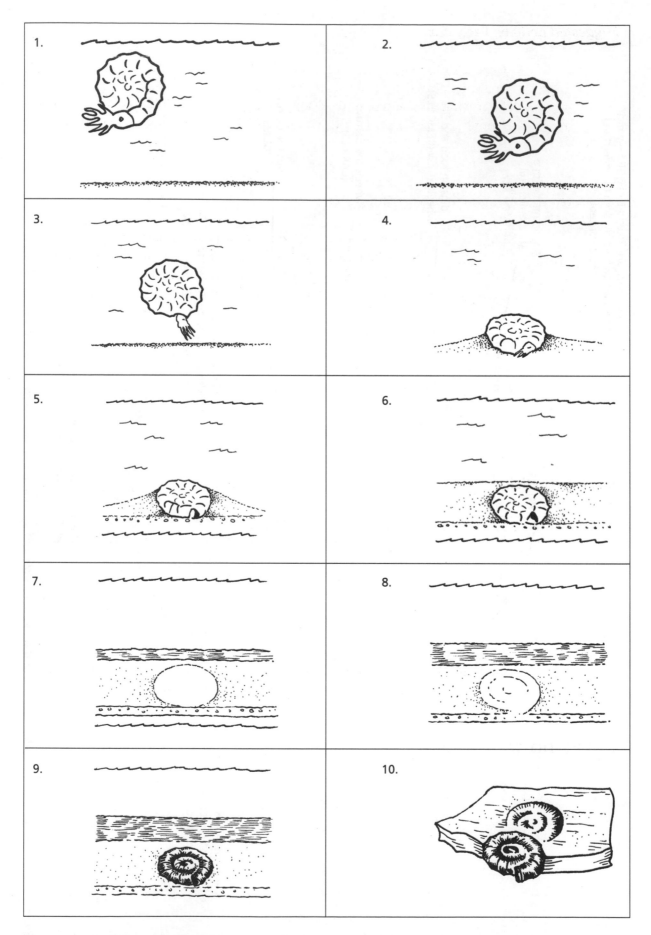

Figure 17 Fossilisation Flicker Book

Suggested activity: Feely box

Once children have gained some familiarity with rocks, a set of samples could be placed in a feely box (a large box with holes cut in the sides, just large enough for hands to reach into to feel – but not see – the samples). Samples might include soil, wood, a piece of fruit or a vegetable as well as rocks.

Suggested activity: 'Stone stores' and pencil pots

Children could display all the larger sorted pebbles of one type in a plastic sweet jar (confectioners are usually happy to give these away) and use the jar as a book end. This then acts as an attractive stone store until the activity is practised again. Alternatively, small pebbles could be set into a thin layer of Polyfilla spread onto a container of a suitable size to hold pencils or paint brushes.

A layer of solvent-free varnish (such as the 'ECOS' range) could then be applied to bring the colours out. Alternatively, if you simply wish to bring the colours out whilst the children are studying them, just dip the pebbles in a bowl of water.

Suggested activity: Where is my partner?   A matching game

Children are given two sets of specimens on separate trays and are asked to match each from one tray with a partner from the other, giving the reasons for their choices. Partners might be: 2 fossils, 2 sedimentary rocks, 2 metamorphic rocks, 2 igneous rocks, 2 jagged rocks, 2 man-made 'rocks', and 2 soils. Any pairing would be acceptable: so long as observations are made, each child can work at their own level.

As a variation for groups working at higher levels, there could be an 'odd man out' or an 'odd pair out' (e.g. a living pair), or some sets of 3 or 4 (e.g. 4 fossils which could be further subdivided into plant and animal fossils).

WHERE DO WE FIND ROCKS?

Children may be able to list some or all of the following:

quarries, cliffs, river beds, road and railway cuttings, mines, caves and tunnels.

Note that all these are rocks that have not yet been broken up into rock fragments to produce loose pebbles, boulders and so on. Children may also mention beaches, which will provide an opportunity to discuss where the sand might have come from, i.e. wearing away of cliffs or land by the sea, and rivers, respectively. Given time, hard rocks do wear away: look for examples of worn steps and try to date them to give an idea of the time taken for rocks to erode.

Suggested activity: Reading with Rocky Rex

As an introduction to the topic, the extract from 'Reading the Rocks' should promote interest and understanding (see pages 97–102).

Reproduced from 'Reading the Rocks', © P.S. Whitehead, published by Rocky Rex Enterprises, 1989. The character 'Rocky Rex' is wholly owned by Rocky Rex Enterprises and may not be used without permission.

'With a name like mine, you won't be surprised to know that I find ROCKS quite entertaining, so that's what I decided to write about.

ROCKS are not always easy to understand, so I'll ask lots of questions to help.

I'll be in a lot of the pictures, as well; I'm a very young Tyrannosaur, only about 2 metres high, so when you see me you will be able to tell the size of things in the pictures.

We're going to have fun in this book, so turn the page and let's get going . . .'

'*Come on then, let's hear about rock.*'

Right, Rocky, first tell us where we find rock. We need to OBSERVE it first.

'*I know the kind you get at the seaside best! It says things like "Bognor" all the way through it.*'

We can do without your silly ideas. But of course, you can see the kind of rock we are really talking about at the seaside, in the cliffs and sticking up out of the beach or the shallow water.

'*You have to be careful. The cliffs often fall down.*'

Yes – that is worth keeping in mind – not just for safety but it comes into our story later on.

'*The rock in these cliffs is all layered. Right on top is a layer of soil, then grass.*'

That is true nearly everywhere – no matter where you are. If you can see under the grass and soil (or concrete and tarmac) you will see rock. It's always there, if you can get to it.

'*So if we want to study rock, we have to go to places where the soil and other things have been taken away?*'

Yes – in some places it is very difficult to look at the rock, but in other places it can be easy. Your sea-cliff was a good place, for example.

'*Here's another good place. There's a river here which has lots of rock showing in its bed. Rivers don't always show rock, though.*'

That's right, sometimes the bed of the river is full of sand and gravel and pebbles. That's part of our story, as well. Of course, you can often find rock sticking out of hillsides, where the soil is very thin, and it helps a lot if nature has EXPOSED the rock for us.

'*Why do some rocks get exposed, when others don't?*'

That is one of the many ways that different rocks vary. They are not all the same. We can say more of that later.

'What can we do if there are no sea-cliffs or river valleys?'

Well, often we can look at rock in places where people have dug holes. Rock has been dug out of the ground for thousands of years, so there are a lot of holes you can see rock in.

'Are they safe?'

Some are and some aren't. Take quarries, for instance. Some quarries have been left for a long time since they were dug. They may be covered with weeds, so you might not see a hole before you fall into it.

Others may have steep faces like the sea-cliff, and they can fall down. That can be dangerous if you are under, and if you are on top.

'I always wear my helmet if there's any chance of anything falling on me.'

Good for you, Rocky.

A working quarry

Of course, if the quarry is still in use, you can't go in to look at the rock without asking first. You should also keep well away from any of the machines.

'Even rivers sometimes belong to people.'

Yes – in fact just about EVERYWHERE belongs to someone. You should ask before you go looking at rocks.

'Are there other places we can see rocks?'

Of course, there are places like caves and mines where people can see lots of rock – but again, they can be very dangerous, and you can't go there often.

'I know where I can see lots of rocks in places you haven't told us about.'

Where, Rocky?

'In buildings. Lots of churches, banks, shops and houses have rock.'

Yes, Rocky, and in fact there are very few buildings that are not made of rock.

'No! Most are made of brick or concrete.'

Oh yes, but what are brick and concrete? In fact they are made of rock.

'That's a good story. I want to hear more about that.'

You don't believe that concrete is made of rock, Rocky?

Slate roof

Rough stone

Dressed stone on corners

Welsh farmhouse built of local rocks

'Sounds unlikely. It's man-made.'

Yes, but what from? If you ask at any factory, and find out what they use to make things, you can try to trace what those things were made from, and so on.

For example, BUILDING MATERIALS like concrete, bricks and glass can all be traced back to something that was dug out of the ground. They don't grow on trees, you know, Rocky.

'Aha, caught you out! Wood DOES grow on trees.'

Yes, but where does the tree get the materials it needs to make itself?

'Out of the soil . . . oh, you win again.'

In fact, if you think about it there are very few things that we can get from anywhere other than the Earth.

'We use a lot of plastic now. You don't have plastic mines.'

Sorry, Rocky, but we do really. Most of them are called OIL WELLS.

Oil rig

'Is plastic made from oil then? I thought oil was just to make petrol and things like that.'

Yes, oil – and coal – can be made into lots of things. You don't have to burn them. In fact, a lot of people think it's a bit wasteful to burn away all those useful chemicals that can be made into so many other things.

'We burn them to get ENERGY. So we get that from the Earth as well as actual things.'

Yes, there are a lot of ways of getting energy from the Earth, although we get most of the energy from the SUN originally.

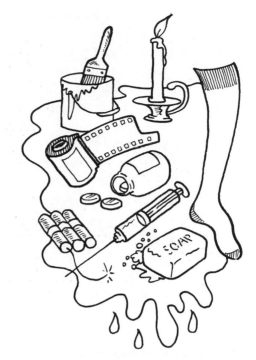

Some things made from coal and oil

'What about metals? We find those in the Earth as well, don't we?'

We do, Rocky. Most of them are not just dug up as lumps of metal. Mainly the stuff we dig up is an ORE. We have to get the metal out, and that can be very difficult, and use lots of energy.

The first metals that people used were things that did lie around as lumps sometimes, like copper, gold or silver.

Things like iron need a pretty hot fire, and some other things, to get them out, so people didn't use them until later.

Cornish tin mine

Some metals need so much energy to get them out of their ores that no-one could do it until quite recently, using electricity.

For example, there was no actual aluminium extracted from its ore until the mid-nineteenth century. Even then, for quite a long time, it was very rare and expensive. People who owned aluminium knives and forks had to be rich, so for a while it was a status symbol.

'I never knew we got so much from rocks.'

Of course, we need to know about rocks for other reasons than just getting things out of them.

'I think some of them are very pretty.'

Yes – and of course lots of them are used as jewellery, like diamonds.

'And because the Earth is made of lots of different types of rock, we need to know what type is under a building before we put it up.'

Very true, Rocky – people have realised that for a long time. After all, it's in the Bible, about the man who builds his house on sand, and gets it washed away.

'People can still have their houses fall down because they didn't think about that.'

Yes, they worry a lot about the number of rooms, the size of the garage and so on, but they don't find out what is under the foundations.

'I think that we are going to find a lot of surprising things as we look at rocks.'

Summary

Rocks are found everywhere: the Earth is made of rocks. In most places, rocks are hidden by soil, grass or buildings. We can study rocks in sea-cliffs, river valleys and quarries. Underground rocks can be seen in caves and mines. When we go to look at rocks, we must follow SAFETY RULES. Rock is the source of nearly everything we use, and we stand our buildings on it.

Fill in the gaps in these sentences:

1   Rocks are often hidden from sight by_____, _____ or _____.

2   Plastic is made mainly from _____ and coal.

3   We get _____ from ores.

4   Rocks are extracted from the Earth in quarries and _____.

5   Rocks can fall from cliffs, so it's wise to wear a _____ when walking beneath them.

Choose your answers from the following list:

oil,   metals,   helmet

soil,   mines,

buildings,   plants

Suggested activity: Model of hidden rocks

You can make a model using plaster or Plasticine to represent the rocks underlying a locality that is being studied. The Plasticine will illustrate how rock is exposed in cliffs and quarries but is hidden by soil elsewhere. You can represent the soil by using real soil samples, sprinkled on Plasticine.

What happens when you go very deep in the earth?

It gets so hot deep inside the Earth (several hundred degrees centigrade) that even rocks melt. (Remind the children that rocks don't melt even when placed in a hot camp fire.) The Earth is made of three layers: the apple analogy below is a useful way of remembering these.

Suggested activity: The Earth's construction

Make a Plasticine model of the Earth, with the core represented by red Plasticine (red, to suggest it's very hot), the mantle by orange and the crust green, then slice it open to show the layers inside.

The Earth's structure: Apple analogy

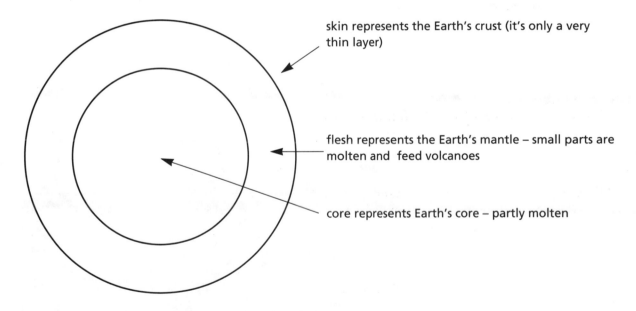

skin represents the Earth's crust (it's only a very thin layer)

flesh represents the Earth's mantle – small parts are molten and feed volcanoes

core represents Earth's core – partly molten

How and where do rocks form?

Suggested activity: This is your life

Children can tell the life history of a pebble they have chosen. Beach pebbles are ideal for the activity. This provides an opportunity to assess the children's grasp of the concepts of weathering, erosion, transport, deposition, geological time, and so on. Use the photocopiable sheet on page 106.

THIS IS YOUR LIFE

Choose your favourite pebble.

You are going to write its life history.

Describe your pebble. How does it feel and look?

Can you think of a good name for it?

See if you can imagine what adventures it had!

(Can you see any chips, scratches or cracks?
Do you think earthquakes, floods, storms at sea or frost might
have caused them?)

Do you think it has travelled far?

Where do you think it lived?

How old do you think it is?

Now you might like to add some pictures

Something geological is cooking! Teacher's background

Children could 'make' rocks with the teacher's help.

Table 13 Analogies between food and rocks

Food analogy	Geological equivalent
Rock buns – dried fruit pebbles cemented together by cake mixture (A non-edible alternative is Polyfilla and pebbles or sand or shells)	Sedimentary (broken and cemented) rocks
Biscuits made by using a rolling pin	Metamorphic (squashed and baked) rocks are hardened by baking and pressure
Toffee – melted sugar and fat. THE TEACHER MUST CARRY OUT THIS EXPERIMENT!	Igneous rocks 'once melted'. Formed by cooling of hot liquid which then solidifies.
Jelly made in an animal mould	Fossil casts (original shape) and moulds (negative of shape)
Toasted cheese sandwiches	Rock layering – making a sandwich a layer at a time. Toasting = metamorphism – some layers melt (cheese), others go hard (bread)
Eggs cooked by frying, scrambling or whisking for an omelette or meringue	The appearance of rocks varies with the conditions in which they form. For example, clay, mudstone, shale and slate are all chemically very similar. Increasing pressure forces out water so that clay becomes mudstone, then shale, and then, under intense pressure, the shale eventually becomes slate. The greater the pressure, the less water present and the harder the rock.

Methods of food preservation
 	
    freezing
    pickling
    bottling
    drying
 	
The presence of bacteria would lead to decay in conditions of low acidity and high temperature where there is oxygen and water
	Fossil preservation
	
	    e.g. fossil mammoths in Siberia
	    e.g. ancient man in peat bogs (acid)
	    e.g. ammonites waterlogged on sea bed
	    e.g. mummified fossils in deserts

WHAT USE DO ROCKS HAVE?

If materials have a relatively low value, they will usually be extracted at the surface, i.e. by quarrying or open-cast mining methods. Where higher value deposits (in quantity or quality) exist, it may be worth extracting them by mining (see page 00). Some materials extracted may be used in their original form, whereas others will be raw materials for manufacturing industry. The activity on page 109 helps children to distinguish raw materials from manufactured products. To run this activity you will need two trays of samples, for example:

Tray 1: Raw material	Tray 2: Manufactured product
clay	bricks and tiles
sand	glass
coal	nylon
oil	plastic
limestone	cement
iron ore	stainless steel

ACTIVITY: MATCHING MATERIALS

1   See if you can sort the materials into two groups:
those which are in their natural form (we call these raw materials) and those that have been altered in a factory (we call these manufactured products).

2   Can you say why you believe the materials belong to that group?

3   Now see if you can match the raw material with its product. List your findings in a table like this:

Raw material	Manufactured product

Suggested activity: Matching materials and uses (for materials used in raw form)

Children could be asked to match the words with the specimen, for example:

Material	Use
marble	ornamental
slate	roofing
quartz	regulating pulse in watch batteries
rock salt	cooking, melting ice on roads
diamond	gemstone, cutting e.g. on drill bits
basalt	aggregate for wearing course of roads (i.e. chippings on surface)

Suggested activity: Clay sedimentation test

The simple experiment on page 111 is an enjoyable way of discovering whether your local clay will make good tiles, bricks or pottery.

Figure 18 Clay sedimentation test
(Reproduced by permission of the Intermediate Technology Development Group)

A simple method of determining how much clay a sample of soil contains, and hence whether it is suitable for making bricks. Try for yourself the test that is helping people in the Third World to make their own bricks.

TRY THIS TEST YOURSELF

To find out whether the soil where you live would be suitable for making bricks simply follow the instructions below.

Place this card against an empty bottle and fill with soil to the level suggested. Then fill with water to the desired level. Add a pinch of salt and shake well. Leave for several hours.

ANALYSING YOUR RESULTS

After this time the soil will have separated into layers. The heaviest sand particles will settle to the bottom of the bottle first, the finer ones above and the finest clay will settle last. On top there will be the water. After the soil has settled, use the percentage gauge on the test sheet to find out the level of sand to clay. In the Third World, the brickmakers use jam jars to carry out the test. We have used a standard bottle, so that everyone can try it.

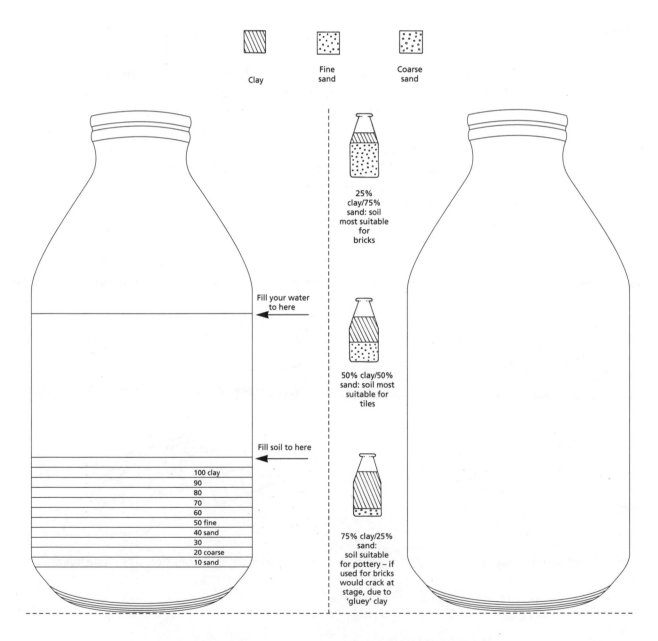

This page can be photocopied onto card. Fold along the dotted lines.

WHAT MATERIALS ARE USED LOCALLY?

Children could investigate the materials of which the school or other local buildings are made and note the change of materials used over time due to improved transport, changing fashions and trading patterns.

Where do these materials come from?

Older buildings tend to be made from locally quarried materials; while modern ones tend to be made of mass-produced manufactured materials. Study of local buildings is a fruitful exercise. An accessible source of information about building stone 'belts' and associated buildings is the Reader's Digest Atlas, and many secondary school atlases also have this information.

What happens to the quarries and mines after they are closed?

Older quarries make good nature reserves and have potential as adventure playgrounds, parks and for other uses, e.g. the National Centre for Alternative Technology, in slate quarries near Machynlleth. However, with steep faces the danger of instability and consequent rockfalls is always there, though the danger diminishes with time as rocks fall, so the slope becomes gentler. Old mines often cause pollution as water flowing through the old workings or spoil heaps washes out chemicals such as lead and acids. Consequently the health of humans and wildlife alike is affected if there are no controls. The Environment Agency monitors this.

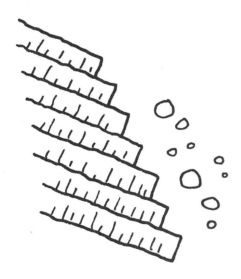

Initial slope profile

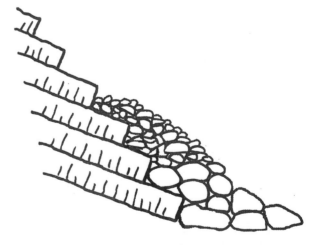

Profile after rockfalls: gentler scree slope builds up at base

Suggested activities: Rock around the house

Use the activity sheets on pp. 00 – 00 to help children learn about how many different materials are used in house-building.

Objectives: To understand that the raw materials for many everyday objects come from rocks.

Introduce the activity by discussing the rocks used to build the classroom.

A variety of worksheets has been suggested, so use the one most suitable for your children or, better still, get them to draw their own.

Table 14 illustrates some of the types of materials used in buildings.

Display: A large picture of a house could be linked by ribbons to the actual rocks used.

You will need:

Copies of house or kitchen worksheet (or children's own drawings);reference books.

HOW MIGHT YOU END THE TOPIC?

The following activity can be photocopied for use in end-of-unit assessments.

Teachers' background

The activity on page 123 allows children to use their imagination, knowledge, and skills of scientific enquiry to decide what they'd build their home from. Their attention could be drawn to the fact that wood, in addition to the rock resources in Table 14, is still a critical component of most houses. Other specimens might be added, depending on what is found locally or has been investigated previously.

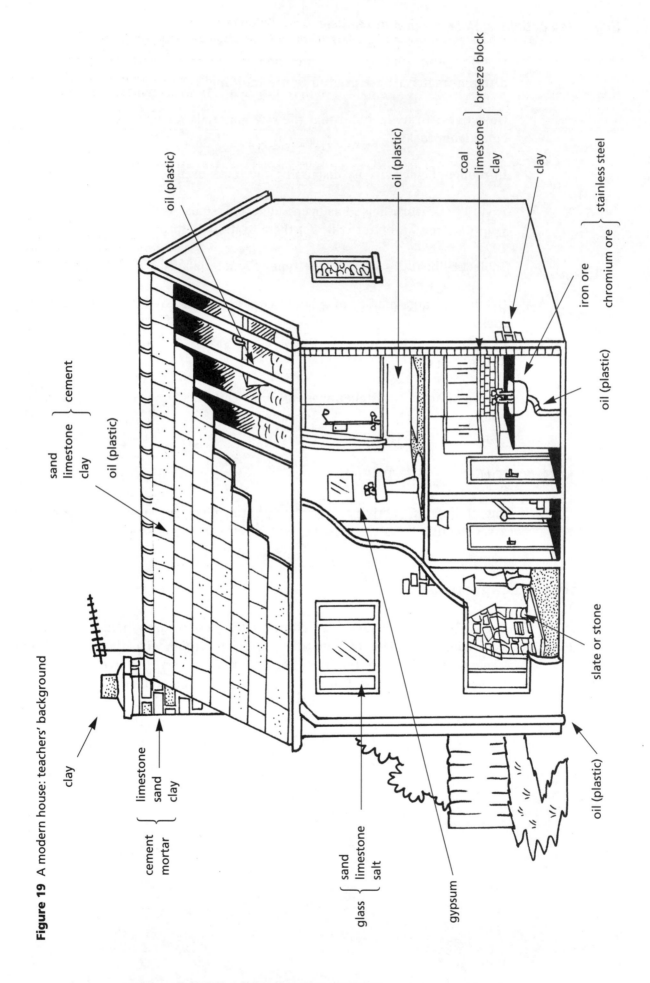

Figure 19 A modern house: teachers' background

oil (plastic)

oil (plastic)

sand ⎱
limestone ⎰ cement
clay

oil (plastic)

clay

cement ⎱ limestone
mortar ⎰ sand
clay

glass ⎱ sand
⎰ limestone
salt

gypsum

coal
limestone ⎱ breeze block
clay

clay

iron ore ⎱ stainless steel
chromium ore ⎰

oil (plastic)

slate or stone

oil (plastic)

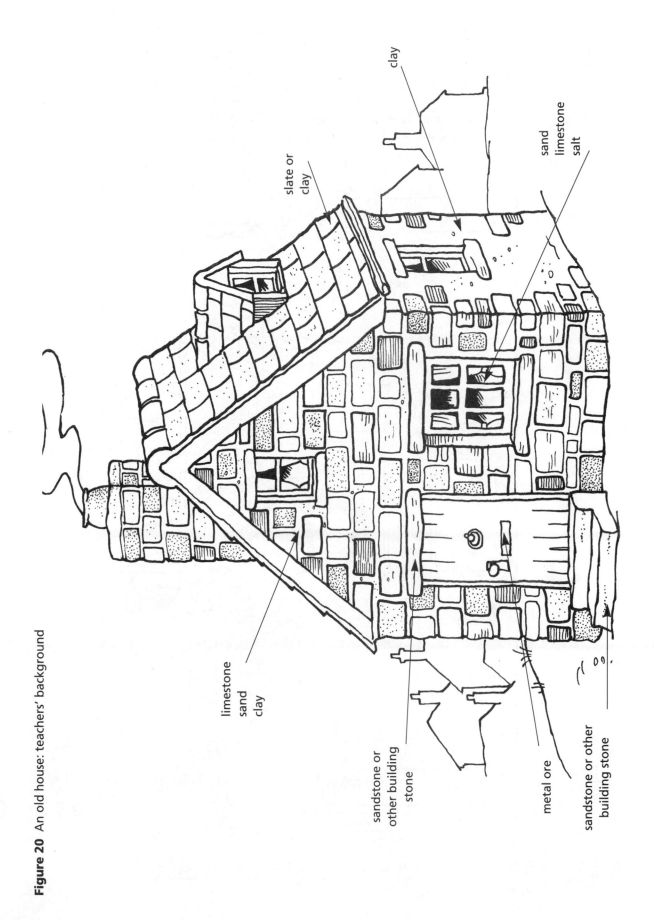

Figure 20 An old house: teachers' background

slate or clay

clay

sand
limestone
salt

limestone
sand
clay

sandstone or other building stone

metal ore

sandstone or other building stone

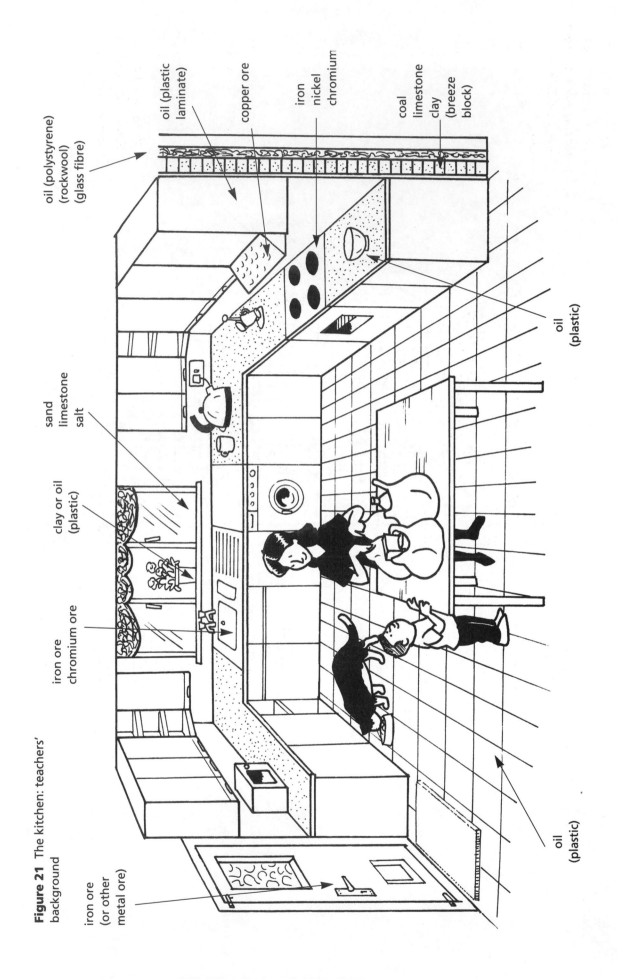

Figure 21 The kitchen: teachers'
background

oil (polystyrene)
(rockwool)
(glass fibre)

oil (plastic laminate)

copper ore

iron
nickel
chromium

coal
limestone
clay
(breeze block)

sand
limestone
salt

clay or oil (plastic)

iron ore
chromium ore

iron ore
(or other metal ore)

oil (plastic)

oil (plastic)

ACTIVITY: ROCK AROUND THE HOUSE

A modern house

How many different rocks or minerals were used to build this house?

How many labels can you fill in on the picture?

No wonder we need so much oil!

How many different rocks can houses be made from?

Can you label other things that come from rocks and minerals?

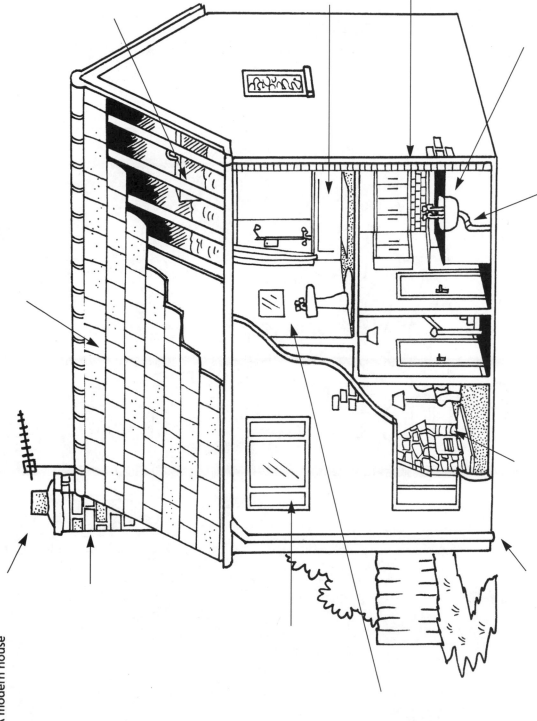

How many different rocks or minerals were used to build this house?

How many labels can you fill in on the picture?

How many different rocks can houses be made from?

Can you label other things that come from rocks and minerals?

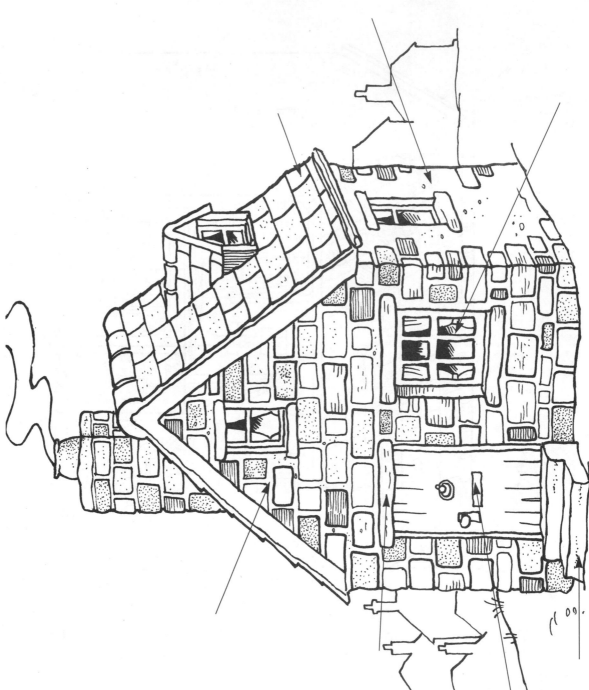

An old house

How many different rocks or minerals were used to build this house?

How many labels can you fill in on the picture?

No wonder we need so much oil!

How many different rocks can houses be made from?

Can you label other things that come from rocks and minerals?

The kitchen

ACTIVITY: BUILD YOUR OWN HOME!

Look at the materials that you have been given: they have all been taken out of the Earth's crust. You are to choose from these materials those which you'd like to build your own home from. You'll probably want to set up some businesses to manufacture the products you need. If you'd like to test any of the materials to find out if they're suitable, ask your teacher.

Try to use natural materials which are environmentally friendly.

Now fill in your decisions on the table below:

What I'd use (name and number of specimen)	What I'd use it for	Why I'd use it

Table 14 Types of rock and their uses

Suitable specimens	How they might use it	Why they might use it
1. Slate	roofing	impermeable
2. Clay	making tiles and bricks	impermeable and cheap
3. Limestone	making cement	with sand and water to make mortar to hold walls together
	making concrete	with sand, gravel and water to make concrete floors
	making limewash	a cheap and environmentally friendly type of paint
4. Gravel	making concrete	see 3 above
	making drains and soakaways	permeable so water flows through it
	making driveways and paths	cheaper than tarmac and permeable
5. Sand	making mortar	see 3 above
	making glass	transparent, to allow light in
6. Iron ore	making steel	strength
7. Oil	making plastics for gutters, window frames etc.	impermeable, lightweight, rot proof

TEACHING ROCKS IN THE CONTEXT OF PLACE STUDIES

The table below gives an example of how you can use the topic rocks as part of a scheme of work on place studies, at Key Stages 1 and 2. Most schools will be located in densely populated areas where the underlying rocks tend to be sedimentary. However, in Table 15 columns one and two may need to be transposed for some schools. At KS2 rocks should be tied in with the study of economic activity.

Table 15 Teaching rocks at KS1 and 2

	Local area	Contrasting UK locality	EDC locality
KS1	Investigation of an exposure of rock in a natural, dug or artificial site in school grounds or nearby.	Hard (igneous or metamorphic) rocks in upland areas such as Dartmoor and many parts of other national parks. OR	e.g. Ladakh in the Himalayas, mountains formed by great heat and pressure therefore rocks are hard igneous and metamorphic types, or St Lucia.
	Wider local area	**Contrasting UK locality**	**EDC locality**
KS 2	Study of local quarry or mine. In densely populated areas sand and gravel pits or coal mines tend to be or were more common.	Quarrying of e.g. granite or slate for ornamental purposes. Conflict of interest in national parks.	e.g. Ladakh: hard rocks therefore slopes steep and soils erode easily so terraces are built to hold the soil.

Teaching packs on *Ladakh* and *St Lucia* are available from the Geographical Association, 343 Fulwood Road, Sheffield, S10 3BP.

Other active zones of the Earth's crust where the ever-popular subject of earthquakes and volcanoes can be studied in an EDC lie in the Andes as featured in the '*Mountain Child pack*' (KS2/3) £15 + £2 p&p available from Greenlight Publications, Cherry Grove, Llanycefn, Clynderwen, Pembrokeshire SA60 7LL. Tel: 01347 563403.

RECOMMENDED TEACHING RESOURCES

Although your main resource will be specimens, ideas for their use are to be found in:-

1. *Exploring Earth Science* (1992) Very well designed. Enjoyable activities. Science Centre, Lewis Road, Northampton, NN5 7BJ. (Tel: 01604 756134.)
2. *Rocks Around You* (1990) Hobsons Publishing £2-95. Very useful resource book but designed for KS3, excellent value.
3. RTZ, 6 St. James's Square, London, SW1Y 4LD offer a number of free or cheap good quality resources. Recommended are: *My World of Minerals and Metals* (KS2/3), *Mineral Samples Pack* and *The Earth's Resources – Metals* (for KS3 but a useful background covers environmental themes too).

4. PEST (Primary Earth Science Teaching) a supplement to *Teaching Earth Science*, the quarterly journal of the Earth Science Teachers' Association. Membership: S. Rogers, Middledyke Lane, Cottingham, N. Humberside.
5. RTZ, *Natural Resources from the Earth*, SCIP 1993.
6. *Earth Science for Primary Teachers – An inset handbook*, NCC 1993.
7. A geological club for youngsters – ROCKWATCH – membership at £5, guaranteed to provide fun like its sister WATCH projects. Details: 'Rockwatch', The Green, Witham Park, Waterside South, Lincoln. (Tel: 01522 544400.)
8. Eyewitness Science Guide: *How the Earth Works*, John Farnden, Dorling Kindersley (1992).
9. Recommended efficient supplier of wide range of geographical resources: Geo supplies 16 Station Road, Chapeltown, Sheffield, S30 4XH. (Tel: 01142 455746.)

PLACES TO VISIT

The National Stone Centre – a recently opened £1 million museum, Ravenstar Road, Wirkworth, Derbyshire, DE4 4FR, is well worth visiting. It's based in 6 disused limestone quarries, has a free trail, conducted tours, exhibition shop, old lead mines, volcanics, etc. Strongly recommended. (Tel: 01624 824833.)

QUARRY VISITS

Enquiries to the Press Officer, BACMI, 156 Buckingham Palace Road, London SW1 9TR. (Tel: 0207 730 8194.)

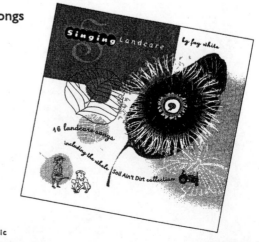